Women of Steel and Stone

22 Inspirational Architects, Engineers, and Landscape Designers

ANNA M. LEWIS

CHICAGO
REVIEW
PRESS

Copyright © 2014, 2017 by Anna M. Lewis
All rights reserved
First hardcover edition published 2014
First paperback edition published 2017
Published by Chicago Review Press, Incorporated
814 North Franklin Street
Chicago, Illinois 60610

ISBN 978-1-61374-508-3 (hardcover)
ISBN 978-1-61373-667-8 (paperback)

The Library of Congress has cataloged the hardcofer edition as follows:
Lewis, Anna M.
   Women of steel and stone : 22 inspirational architects, engineers, and landscape
designers / Anna M. Lewis. — First edition.
      pages cm — (Women of action)
   Summary: "Reporting on a range of historical and contemporary female builders
and designers, this educational book strives to inspire a new generation of girls
in the disciplines of science, technology, engineering, and math. With many of
the profiles set against the backdrop of such landmark events as the women's
suffrage and civil rights movements and the Industrial Revolution, and with
original interviews from a number of current architects and engineers, this book
provides inspiration and advice directly to young women by highlighting positive
examples of how a strong work ethic, perseverance, and creativity can overcome
life's obstacles. Each profile focuses on the strengths, passions, and interests
each woman had growing up; where those traits took them; and what they
achieved. Sidebars on related topics, source notes, and a bibliography make this an
invaluable resource for further study"— Provided by publisher.
   Includes bibliographical references and index.
   ISBN 978-1-61374-508-3 (hardback)
   1. Women architects—Biography—Juvenile literature. 2. Women engineers—
Biography—Juvenile literature. 3. Women landscape architects—Biography—
Juvenile literature. 4. Women—Vocational guidance—Juvenile literature. I. Title.

   NA1997.L49 2014
   720.92'52—dc23
   [B]

                                                2013027049

Cover and interior design: Sarah Olson
Front cover photos: (top) Denise Scott Brown (VSBA); (bottom, from left to right)
house by Anna Wagner Keichline (courtesy of Nancy Jane Perkins, FIDSA);
building by Zaha Hadid (©2012 by Iwan Baan); Brooklyn Bridge (Library of
Congress LC-D4-12702); a San Diego park by Martha Schwartz (Martha Schwartz
Partners)

Printed in the United States of America
5 4 3 2 1

To my dear husband, Robert; my wildly creative children, Emily, Hayden, and Everett; and my forever friends—thanks for holding my hand along the way.

To my father, a consulting engineer for over 50 years, who passed the day before I started writing this book—you would have loved to read it.

And, to all the women profiled in these pages who didn't listen to "No" and pursued their passions. Here's to the women who shaped our world, and those who will build our future.

"Every great dream begins with a dreamer. Always remember, you have within you the strength, the patience, and the passion to reach for the stars to change the world."

—Harriet Tubman

"What would life be if we had no courage to attempt anything?"

—Vincent van Gogh

CONTENTS

PART THREE: LANDSCAPE ARCHITECTS

INTRODUCTION

THE WOMEN WHO helped build the world we live in—female architects, engineers, and landscape architects—had strong wills that helped them break through into professions at a time when women were not welcome or sometimes were not even allowed. These women had strengths, passions, and interests as they were growing up that led them to accomplish amazing achievements. They were all determined women who wanted to create, whether it was a building, a bridge, or a beautiful environment. Most of these spirited women saw the problems they faced entering male-dominated fields more as stumbling blocks or challenges than as outright discrimination. With a few exceptions, the support of their families helped them reach their goals. The women's suffrage (right to vote) movement, the civil rights movement, social reform, America's industrial leaders, and the Roaring Twenties all influenced their diverse life stories.

Women have always played an important role in the creation of houses and buildings. In the hunter-gatherer days, women tended to the home while men went off to hunt. From teepee to cave to log cabin, women have always worked to create safe, nurturing, and healthy environments for their families and communities, and there is early evidence that shows women assuming the role of builder. In 16th-century France, Katherine Briçonnet designed and supervised the building of the Chateau de Chenonceau between 1513 and 1524, while her husband was away fighting at war. In 17th-century England, 19-year-old Lady Elizabeth Wilbraham traveled and studied architecture in the Netherlands and Italy while on her honeymoon. She later set up an architectural office and designed Wotton House in Buckinghamshire and possibly 400 other buildings. Sir Christopher Wren, now known as England's greatest architect, may have studied under her and created 18 churches with the help of her designs before he went on to build more than 50 churches, including St. Paul's Cathedral in London.

In *Families and Farmhouses in Nineteenth-Century America*, author Sally McMurry presents many home plans designed by women which were published in 19th-century farm journals. The 1847 house plan by Matilda Howard of Zanesville, Ohio, won the $20 prize from the Committee on Farm Dwellings for the New York State Agricultural Society. Mrs. Howard's design provided detailed instructions on site and room placement, materials, and cost. Mrs. Howard explained, "In the construction of this plan, it has been my object to combine utility and beauty, as far as practicable with the labor-saving principle."

After Harriet Beecher Stowe wrote *Uncle Tom's Cabin* in 1852, she and her sister, Catharine, wrote *The American Woman's Home* in 1869. Their book lays out the domestic concerns of the 19th century and details a house plan with particular attention paid to areas often ignored by male designers of the 19th century, such as the kitchen. Various chapters concern the need for exercise, both physical and mental, fresh air, gardening, hygiene, clothing reform/removing binding corsets, and the ventilation and heating of the home.

In the late 19th century, women from middle-income families (if they worked outside the home) were typically expected to enter nursing, teaching, or writing professions. In her popular self-help book *What Can a Woman Do?*, Mrs. M. L. Rayne wrote about the careers that were socially acceptable for a woman. They included medicine, law, agriculture, manufacturing, business, dressmaking, education, and the arts. Careers in architecture, engineering, and landscape architecture were not mentioned. Women from wealthy families were told to use their extra energies by doing charity work. The medical community in 1900 even gave excess energy and overuses of intellect a name: "neurasthenia," or nervousness.

The neurasthenia cure for men was to send them out west to rope cattle, hunt, and hang out with cowboys. A few men who went west for the cure were writer Mark Twain, painter Thomas Eakins, and Theodore Roosevelt. Meanwhile, the cure for women was for private doctors to seclude them, possibly in bed, with no visitors, no books, and a bland diet. This was the prescription for reformer Jane Addams and writer Edith Wharton.

In 1900, when 29-year-old Martha Brookes Hutcheson decided to enter the new program in landscape design at the Massachusetts Institute of Technology (MIT), her parents begged her to change her mind, for fear that her decision would affect their social standing. They even offered to send her to Europe, to allow her to design their family estate. But Martha said, "I was fired with the desire . . . in spite of the fact that it was considered almost social suicide and distinctly matrimonial suicide for a woman to enter any profession." Martha ultimately chose to attend MIT—though she circled the block three times before getting the courage to climb the steps to the university.

The government was indirectly instrumental in changing the role of women in architecture and related fields thanks to the Morrill Act, created in 1862 and signed by Abraham Lincoln. The Morrill Act granted government land to colleges for free. Although the Morrill Act did not require that institutions open their doors to women, by 1890, every state included the admission of women in its land grant charter. This enabled women to get college degrees to start working professionally in the areas of architecture, engineering, and landscape architecture, among other fields. Soon thereafter, women began making headway in those industries. In 1873, Mary L. Page became the first woman to earn an architecture degree from the University of Illinois. In 1890, Sophia Hayden became the first woman graduate from MIT's four-year architecture program. In 1904, Marian Coffin graduated from MIT as a special student from the landscape architecture program. In 1905, Nora Stanton Blatch Barney became the first woman to receive a degree in civil engineering from Cornell University.

An article in the 1901 *New-York Daily Tribune* titled "Occupations of Women: What the Field of Architecture Offers to the Well Trained, Practical Woman" reads:

> It must be obvious that women have a more intimate knowledge of the requirements of a home than men usually have. They know of necessity why bedrooms should be properly partitioned, not merely divided by portieres, which leave the occupant of each room at the mercy of every trifling noise in the other. Their personal experience teaches them that fully one-half of the comfort of a house or apartment depends upon the closet room. They would never think of building a small apartment house in such a way that "butcher and baker and candlestick

maker" must carry their goods up the front stairs—as I have seen done.

The architect, engineer, and landscape architect all work hand in hand to create a building and its environment. In 1893, respected art and architecture critic Mariana Van Rensselaer brought new recognition to the garden and defined the landscape architect as "a gardener, an engineer, and an artist, who like an architect considers beauty and utility together." In an article written by turn-of-the-20th-century landscape architect Beatrix Farrand titled "The Garden in Relation to the House," she explained that "the arts of architecture and landscape gardening are sisters . . . not antagonists. . . . The work of the architect and landscape gardener should be done together from the beginning . . . not, as too often happens, one crowding the other out."

Working in concert, the architect, the engineer, and the landscape architect build our world, whether steel beam by steel beam or stone by stone. Women throughout history have made and continue to make increasingly important contributions to this realm, and it is both vital and fascinating to look back at women's history, while looking forward to the amazing architectural achievements sure to come.

PART ONE

ARCHITECTS

ARCHITECTURE WAS FIRST recognized as a profession in the United States in 1857. At first, students learned through apprenticeship or study in Europe. The Massachusetts Institute of Technology School of Architecture and Planning offered the first formal architectural curriculum in the United States, followed by the University of Pennsylvania in 1868, and the University of Illinois at Urbana-Champaign in 1870. In 1871, Cornell University began offering the first four-year program in architecture, and Margaret Hicks became its first woman graduate in 1878. The US census listed only one woman architect in 1870. Twenty years later, in 1890, there were 22 women architects declared. By the 1900 census, there were 100 women listed. The first women architects, such as Louise Bethune, were trained in architectural offices. Many others worked with their husbands, but the women's work was not always recognized because their husbands alone signed the architectural drawings.

In January 1898, 12 architects took the first licensing exam in Chicago's city hall, in response to the world's first licensing law passed by the Illinois General Assembly in June 1897. Marion Mahony was one of those 12 architects, and she passed.

In 1913, Lois Lilley Howe and Eleanor Manning established one of the few architectural firms of its time run solely by women. Howe did not mince words when it came to the prospect of making a living as an architect: "As a means of livelihood for a woman, architecture is precarious and unadvisable, unless she has wonderful natural capacity combined with great tenacity of purpose, to which may be added exceptional opportunities." She went on to describe the prejudice against women as "so great as to make it almost impossible for a woman to learn her trade." Nonetheless, she worked to support younger women entering the profession by offering apprenticeships in her firm.

Today, about 40 percent of architecture students are women. The Bureau of Labor Statistics and a 2009 American Institute of Architects (AIA) Survey state that in 2008, there were 141,200 women architects employed in the United States, and 16 percent growth is expected by 2018. According to studies conducted in 2012 by the Bureau of Labor Statistics and Georgetown University's Center on Education and the Workforce, more than 21 percent of architects are self-employed, which is three times higher than the self-employment seen in other fields.

In the last decade or so, there has been increasingly more discussion about the role of the woman architect. Created in 2002, the nonprofit Beverly Willis Architecture Foundation has been instrumental in promoting women architects in the industry. When Mattel introduced Architect Barbie in 2011, everyone looked around and asked, "Where *are* the women architects?" This book furthers the conversation about women in architecture; it brings to light women's contributions to the field and will hopefully enlighten and ignite the aspirations of a new generation of designers, dreamers, and creators who will build our world to never-before-seen heights.

AMERICA'S TOP ARCHITECTURE SCHOOLS 2013

Based on responses to a 2013 survey sent to 282 American architectural and architectural/engineering offices employing more than 40,000 professionals, *Architectural Record* magazine compiled the following list of America's top architecture schools. Bear in mind that the ranking of these schools is rather subjective; the schools vary greatly in terms of their academic and technical strengths. Currently, there are 125 schools in the United States offering professional graduate and undergraduate architectural degree programs.

Top 10 Architecture Undergraduate Programs

1. Cornell University
2. Southern California Institute of Architecture
3. Rice University
4. Syracuse University
5. California Polytechnic State University
6. University of Texas at Austin
7. Virginia Polytechnic Institute and State University
7. Rhode Island School of Design
9. Iowa State University
10. Auburn University

Top 10 Architecture Graduate Programs

1. Harvard University
2. Columbia University
3. Yale University
4. Massachusetts Institute of Technology
5. Cornell University
6. Southern California Institute of Architecture
7. University of Virginia
8. University of California, Berkeley
9. Washington University in St. Louis
10. University of Cincinnati

LOUISE BETHUNE

Paving the Way

As a young child, Jennie Louise "Lulu" Blanchard was teased by a male classmate, who jokingly proclaimed, "Lulu, girls can't be architects." The teasing was later recounted in the 1893 book *A Woman of the Century*: "A caustic remark had previously turned her attention in the direction of architecture, and an investigation, which was begun in a spirit of playful self-defense, soon became an absorbing interest." That interest turned into determination, and Lulu proved that young man wrong by becoming the first woman architect in America.

Jennie Louise Blanchard Bethune was born on July 21, 1856, in Waterloo, New York. Her older brother died when he was young, leaving Louise the only child of Emma Melona Williams

Louise Bethune.
Chicago Public Library

and Dalson Wallace Blanchard. Dalson's ancestors were French Huguenot refugees, and Melona's family came to America in 1640, landing in Massachusetts from Wales.

Due to her poor health, young Louise was homeschooled until she was 11. She couldn't have had better teachers than her parents: her father was a mathematician and school principal at Waterloo Union School, and her mother was a schoolteacher. When Louise was 12 years old, the family moved to Buffalo, New York, so she could attend Buffalo High School, where she became known as "Lulu" by teachers and classmates. After high school graduation, Louise taught, traveled, and studied for two years in preparation for enrollment at Cornell University.

In 1876, she began work as a draftsman for architect Richard A. Waite and gave up her plans to study architecture in college. She worked from 8:00 AM to 6:00 PM and the pay was low, but she had access to the office library. After five years as a drafter and assistant, she opened her own office in Buffalo. She was only 25 years old, and she was already the first woman architect in America. In December 1881, she married Robert A. Bethune, a former coworker, and he joined her in her architecture practice.

> "Mrs. Bethune refuses to confine herself . . . believing that women who are pioneers in any profession should be proficient in every department."

In the 23 years that the office was open, the firm designed 15 commercial and 8 industrial buildings, many schools, and several other public buildings, including a police station, a church, and a prison. One of Louise's areas of concentration was public schools, though she refused to have her work pigeonholed.

Indeed, an 1893 biography stated that "Mrs. Bethune refuses to confine herself exclusively to that branch, believing that women who are pioneers in any profession should be proficient in every department, and that now at least women architects must be practical superintendents as well as designers and scientific constructors, and that woman's complete emancipation lies in 'equal pay for equal service.'"

Louise opened her architecture firm at an opportune time: Buffalo was expanding its school system, and Louise designed 18 schools in all. Louise and Robert took all commissions that were available to them, and they designed a plant for the Iroquois Door Company, the Erie County Penitentiary women's prison, grandstands for the Queen City Baseball and Amusement Company, and the transformer building that brought electricity from Niagara Falls to the Buffalo trolleys. The late 19th century saw a turn toward new scientific developments in sanitation, ventilation, fireproofing, and function, all of which were elements that Louise incorporated in her designs. The firm implemented innovative techniques and materials in their design for Denton, Cottier & Daniels music store, one of the first structures built of steel-frame construction with fire-resistant concrete slabs. In Louise's school buildings, she designed wide hallways with two fire exits throughout all parts of the school, now a code requirement for all public buildings. Louise also used heavy timbers, layered hardwoods, and brick construction for fireproofing.

Buffalo's Hotel Lafayette in Lafayette Square is Louise's best-known building. It took six years to design and build, and cost a whopping $1 million. When the doors were opened in 1904, the seven-story, 225-room hotel was considered "one of the most perfectly appointed and magnificent hotels in the country." Made of steel frame and concrete, the French Renaissance–style building was designed implementing new fire codes, a very

Hotel Lafayette, Buffalo, New York.
Library of Congress, LC-D4-71141

important safety issue as cities and buildings were growing. Each room in the seven-story building had hot and cold running water and a phone, which were considered luxuries at the turn of the century. The landmark is now on the National Register of Historic Places, and a $35 million rehabilitation project in 2012 has restored the building to its original grace and grandeur.

Louise and Robert had one child, Charles W. Bethune, born in 1883. They employed another architect around the time that their son was born, William L. Fuchs, and made Fuchs a partner in 1890. The firm eventually changed its name to Bethune, Bethune, and Fuchs.

Louise became a member of the Western Association of Architects in 1885 and was elected the first female member of the American Institute of Architects (AIA) in 1888. When both organizations merged, she became a fellow of the AIA.

HENRIETTA DOZIER

The third woman to become a member of AIA was a southerner, Henrietta Dozier. The first female architect in Georgia, Henrietta graduated from MIT in 1899 with a degree in architecture. Her first office was in Atlanta; then, in 1916, she moved her practice to Jacksonville, Florida. Throughout her career, she hid the fact that she was a woman by signing her correspondence and blueprints with various names, such as "Cousin Harry," "Harry," and "H. C. Dozier." During her career, she designed several churches, schools, banks, government buildings, houses, and apartment buildings.

Louise's independent spirit extended beyond the realm of architecture. She bought the first women's bicycle sold in Buffalo, and was a charter member of the Wheeling Division of the Women's Wheel and Athletic Club. Miss Emma Villiaume, the captain of the all-woman Wheeling Club, recapped one of the group's weekly runs to Niagara Falls:

> It was a quarter to four when my alarm clock rang . . . It had been very rainy, and it was hardly light enough to see when I started for the rendezvous, followed by the fears and protests of my family. I found the other five waiting for me, fortified like myself with a cup of coffee and possibly a few crackers, and off we went, making good time out Grant Street and until we reached Military Road. . . . It was then about half-past 11, and after a dinner at the International we rode about Prospect Park, all around the islands and through the sightseeing roads. We all felt that

we had never before seen Niagara so thoroughly, and that it had certainly been a delightful day.

On March 6, 1891, Louise spoke on the subject of women and architecture to the Women's Educational and Industrial Union in Buffalo. Louise's opening statement noted that she had been invited to speak on "Women in Architecture," but she changed the title to "Women *and* Architecture." She explained, "In order to have any topic at all, we must talk of women and architecture, assuming a connection which it is hardly safe to assert."

She felt that at the time there was a need for women doctors and women lawyers; but, she said, "There is no need whatever for a women architect. No one wants her, no one yearns for her, and there is no special line in architecture to which she is better adapted than as a man . . . [the woman architect] has exactly the same work to do as a man. When a woman enters the profession she will be met kindly and will be welcome, but not as a woman, only as an architect." Louise was trying to say that women are no different than men, and she felt there was no need to differentiate between female and male architects. In entering the field of architecture, she asserted, men and women were on equal playing fields.

Louise's discomfort with women's place in the field of architecture came up again during the 1893 World's Columbian Exposition. Held in Chicago, the exposition introduced 27 million visitors to the newest innovations of the time, such as the Ferris wheel, the zipper, Cracker Jack, and many others. Chicago's architects organized and designed the "White City," made up of more than 600 acres of buildings and settings that fueled imaginations for decades. The floor of one hall alone covered 32 acres. The buildings were designed by many pioneers of 20th-century architecture, all of whom were chosen by appointment:

Daniel Burnham, John Root, William Jenny, Louis Sullivan, and others. Two buildings from the 1893 Exposition remain standing today: the Palace of Fine Arts, which now houses Chicago's Museum of Science and Industry, and the World's Congress Auxiliary Building, which houses the Art Institute of Chicago.

Additionally, the fair's 117-member Board of Lady Managers decided to construct a Women's Building to showcase the architectural achievements of women, and they held a competition to select a woman architect for the project.

Louise and many other AIA members boycotted juried competitions—including the competition to design the Women's Building—because the judges were generally inexperienced in

SOPHIA HAYDEN

The woman who won the design competition for the Columbian Exposition's Women's Building was 21-year-old Sophia Hayden. Born in Chile, Sophia was sent to live with her grandparents in America when she was six years old. Sophia was interested in architecture in high school, and she went on to become the first woman to graduate with a degree in architecture from the Massachusetts Institute of Technology (MIT).

The president of the Board of Lady Managers for the exposition was Bertha Palmer, wife of a wealthy dry goods merchant. Sophia soon learned that Mrs. Palmer had invited her high-society friends to donate architectural elements for the building. When Sophia tried to explain to Mrs. Palmer her design for the building and why these random donated elements would not work, Mrs. Palmer fired her. Many architects defended Sophia, but the experience soured her on architecture, and she never returned to it.

WOMEN'S IMPACT AT THE
1893 WORLD'S COLUMBIAN EXPOSITION

The 1893 World's Columbian Exposition was a turning point in the women's movement. The Women's Building, designed by architect Sophia Hayden, showcased and symbolized the importance of women. The vast array of exhibits displayed women's progress from primitive to modern times in the arts, crafts, sciences, education, and labor. The building's library of books written by women contained more 7,000 books from 24 nations.

Over 150,000 people attended the new World's Congress Auxiliary Building, now the Art Institute of Chicago, to participate in the seven-day World's Congress of Representative Women. Five hundred delegates representing 27 countries and 126 organizations attended 81 meetings. More than 330 women, including Susan B. Anthony, Jane Addams, and Elizabeth Cady Stanton, addressed the Congress.

reading architectural plans. This led many judges to champion buildings that ran over-budget and could not be built. Even worse, on occasion, a political favorite would be awarded the contract over a more suitable architect.

The competition was even more insulting given that the winner would receive an award of just $1,000, one-tenth of what each of the men were paid for their "personal artistic services." Plus, some architects may have reduced their fees in order to get appointments, another opposition of AIA guidelines. Louise was the only architect to protest on this issue. In her refusal to compete, she made a plea for equal pay for women. Her

ROSANNAH SANDOVAL

In 2013, at age 23, Rosannah Sandoval achieved the title of youngest licensed architect. Rosannah explains, "Since I can remember, I cared about built things and the way light falls. About color and shapes and simplicity. Before I knew of 'architecture' in the formal sense I was drawn to the action of making and realizing ideas through materials. I began architecture school in Alabama and finished in San Francisco at 18 years old." She's currently an architect in Perkins + Will's San Francisco office.

actions were likely influenced by the women's suffrage activities in upstate New York. The site of the first women's suffrage convention in 1846 was a stone's throw from her hometown of Waterloo, in Seneca Falls, New York. Louise was passionate and outspoken on the broader AIA principles of equal pay and ethical treatment of all architects. She did not need the publicity of the World's Fair commission to validate her work.

Louise was encouraging when she spoke to the Women's Educational and Industrial Union in 1891, and she urged women not to settle for lower-level tasks but to be ambitious—to reach higher and do better. She explained:

The total number of women graduates from the various schools of the country can hardly exceed a dozen, and most of these seem to have renounced ambition with the attainment of a degree, but there are among them a few brilliant and energetic women for whom the future holds great possibilities. There are also a few women drafting in various offices through the country, and the only respect in which they fall below their brothers is in disinclination to familiarize themselves with the practical questions of actual construction. They shirk the brick-and-mortar, rubber-boot, and ladder-climbing period of investigative education, and as a consequence remain at the tracing stage of draftsmanship. There are hardly more successful women draftsmen than women graduates, but the next decade will doubtless give us a few thoroughly efficient architects from their number.

Louise's name was still listed in the business section of the *Buffalo City Directory* until 1910, though she moved into the home of her son in 1907. Louise died on December 18, 1913, at age 57.

LEARN MORE

Buffalo and Erie County Historical Society, Louise Bethune Exhibit Interactive Video Tour, http://buffalovr.com/bech/index.html

The First American Women Architects by Sarah Allaback (University of Illinois Press, 2008)

From Craft to Profession: The Practice of Architecture in Nineteenth-Century America by Mary N. Woods (University of California Press, 1999)

ANNA WAGNER KEICHLINE

Brick by Brick

M AY DEVOTE LIFE TO INDUSTRIAL ART was the splashy head-line for a 1903 *Philadelphia Inquirer* newspaper profile about then-teenager Anna Wagner Keichline. The article read:

> Such a liking has she taken to industrial art that Miss Anna Keichline . . . expects to make it her life study. She has just taken the first prize at the Centre county fair for a card table made of oak and a walnut chest she made with her own hands. They, in quality and finish, compare favor-ably with the work of a skilled mechanic. At her home here she has a workshop complete in every detail, and is in possession of the best outfit of carpenter implements to

Anna Keichline at 14 years old.
Courtesy of Nancy Jane Perkins, FIDSA

be found in the town. She goes to school, but every spare moment is put into her shop.

The photo of Anna that accompanied the article did not resemble a dirty shop boy but a pretty young lady with a big white bow in her hair wearing a white sailor dress.

Anna was born in Bellefonte, Pennsylvania, on May 24, 1889, the youngest child of John and Sarah Wagner Keichline. Anna's ancestors immigrated to America from Germany on the ship *Francis and Elizabeth*, arriving at the Pennsylvania docks in 1742. Her father was a respected attorney in Bellefonte.

As a young girl Anna showed a keen interest in woodworking, and, as the *Inquirer* article pointed out, her parents provided her with all the tools she needed. By the time Anna was 14 years old, she was well known as a skilled craftswoman and had already declared it her career path.

Clearly encouraged in her talents, Anna continued to excel. In 1906, after graduating from Bellefonte High School, she followed her older brother to Pennsylvania State College, where, despite being the only woman in the class, she decided to study mechanical engineering.

The next year, Anna transferred to Cornell University to study architecture. She was full of energy, and she was a member of the drama club as well as the women's basketball team. Anna was also tapped to become a member of Raven and Serpent, an honorary society for junior women, in addition to being elected a junior class officer. During

"I took time to make coffee and sandwiches for the fellows, then they carried my board to the dormitory, where I would draw all night."

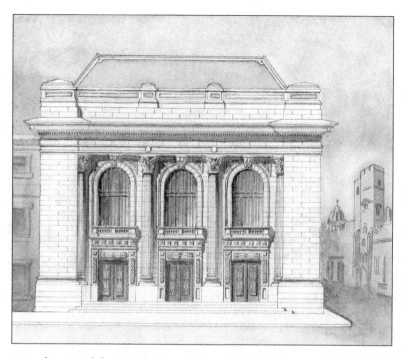

An architectural drawing by Anna Wagner Keichline.
Courtesy of Nancy Jane Perkins, FIDSA

her senior year, she was recognized for outstanding achievement in scholarship, leadership, and public service. Despite all
of her accomplishments, family members recall that there was
some concern that the university would not present Anna with
an actual diploma because she was a woman. Many universities and colleges at the time were giving women "certificates"
instead of diplomas. Anna was so well liked in college that concerned students threatened to protest at the ceremony. To the
relief of all concerned, Anna received her diploma and became
the fifth woman to receive an architecture degree.

Years later Anna was quoted in the *Philadelphia Inquirer*, talking about her college life:

Curtin Street House, Bellefonte, Pennsylvania.
Courtesy of Nancy Jane Perkins, FIDSA

At college we worked, many times, three and four days and nights without stopping; most always in those stretches I took time to make coffee and sandwiches for the fellows, then they carried my board to the dormitory, where I would draw all night. Now after years of practice, I realize that I have never thought of hours, time is divided into jobs, a floor plan, a model, specifications, until the job is done.

Anna's first architectural design was for a school in Milesburg, Pennsylvania. Today her building projects can be found in central Pennsylvania, Ohio, and Washington, DC. In her hometown of Bellefonte, she designed the Plaza Theatre, the Cadillac Garage and Apartments, the Harvey Apartments, and several homes. Other Pennsylvania projects include the Juniata Colony

Country Clubhouse in Mount Union and a Presbyterian church in Mill Hall. For many years, she shared an office with her father in the Temple Court Building.

On the Fourth of July in 1913, Anna led a suffragist parade down Bellefonte's main street. Holding the first banner high in the air, she proudly marched wearing her graduation cap and gown, making a personal statement that all women can receive college degrees. Seemingly, Anna ignored the possibility that her actions could cause her to lose clients.

In 1920, when registration became a requirement to practice architecture in the state, Anna passed the exam, making her the first woman registered as an architect in Pennsylvania.

In addition to her gains as an architect, Anna enjoyed considerable success and recognition as an inventor. Her most notable achievement was the invention of an inexpensive, lightweight clay brick to be used for hollow-wall construction. The K-brick, as it became known, could be filled with insulation or soundproofing materials and had predetermined fracture points for custom fitting at the job site. In her article "Modern Wall Construction," which appeared in the 1932 issue of *Clay-Worker*, Anna wrote about her new technique of building and wall construction, explaining the benefits and history of brick construction and proclaiming that the

The K-brick, patented by Anna Keichline.
Courtesy of Nancy Jane Perkins, FIDSA

country was experiencing the biggest transformation in architecture and construction. The American Ceramic Society honored her for her invention of the K-brick in 1931.

"If [you] should deem it advisable to give me something more difficult or as I wish to say more dangerous, I should much prefer it."

Along with the design patent for the K-brick, Anna received six utility patents: a sink for apartments (1912), a toy (1916), components for kitchen construction (1926), a child's portable partition (1927), a folding bed for apartments (1929), and a ventilation air system (1931).

During World War I, Anna's career was briefly interrupted by a new adventure. In a letter volunteering to help in the war effort, Anna wrote:

With reference to my history, past experiences, etc. Bellefonte High School four years, graduated 1906, one year in Mechanical Engineering at Penn State 1906–1907, Cornell four years in Architecture 1907–1911, office experience and six years independent practice in the general run of work in planning and construction. Am twenty-eight and physically somewhat stronger than the average. Might add that I can operate and take care of a car. The above would suggest a drafting or office job, but if should deem it advisable to give me something more difficult or as I wish to say more dangerous, I should much prefer it.

Anna was fluent in German and could decipher both oral and written communications. The military clearly recognized her exceptional and useful talent, and Anna went on to serve as a special agent for the Military Intelligence Division of the US Army, living in Washington, DC, until the end of the war.

A truly independent woman for her time, Anna owned, drove, and repaired her own car, a Chandler automobile. She was a fan of Abraham Lincoln and fly-fishing. In the December 1936 issue of *American Architects and Architecture*, she was featured in an article titled "Architects and Avocations." The caption next to a photo of Anna fly-fishing read, "Add to the roster of architects who fish for something other than clients the name of Miss A. W. Keichline, Bellefonte, Pennsylvania."

Anna felt that women not only had an innate talent for kitchen design, but for designing the entire home. "The equipment of houses, especially, has been developed by people who seldom have experience using or operating these materials," she pointed out. "Women, as engineers or architects have immense opportunities there. There should be scientifically built houses and this can be done better by women than

Photo of Anna Keichline, part of her application for service in the US Army's Military Intelligence Division.
Courtesy of Nancy Jane Perkins, FIDSA

by men. Indeed this will never be accomplished until women take hold."

Though Anna never married, she was a beloved aunt to her nieces and nephews, who loved her cream-cheese-and-onion sandwiches. Anna died on February 5, 1943. The state of Pennsylvania honored her with an official historical state marker in 2002. It can be found in front of Bellefonte's Plaza Theatre, which she designed and built in 1925.

A dollhouse that Anna made for her nieces and nephews.
Courtesy of Nancy Jane Perkins, FIDSA

LEARN MORE

"Anna Keichline," Association of Women Industrial Designers (AWID), Nancy Perkins, FIDSA, AWID, www.awidweb.com/pages/anna/anna_1.html

Anna Wagner Keichline Exhibit at the Bellefonte Art Museum for Centre County in Bellefonte, Pennsylvania, www.bellefontemuseum.org/Architecture_Design.htm

Design and Feminism: Re-visioning Spaces, Places, and Everyday Things by Joan Rothschild, ed. (Rutgers University Press, 1999)

She Built a Castle

"Every architect who ever worked with Julia Morgan said the only problem with her was that they couldn't live on Hershey bars and coffee even though she did," Morgan North explained about his Aunt Julia. "At midnight, everybody would be famished, so she'd break out a couple of Hershey bars and pass them around, and then start to work again."

This prolific architect with an abundance of energy and determination broke through several barriers and designed more than 700 buildings over 30 years, while simultaneously creating the famous Hearst Castle at San Simeon, California.

Born on January 20, 1872, Julia Morgan was the second child of Charles and Eliza Morgan. She grew up in Oakland,

Julia Morgan.
The Granger Collection, New York

California—at that time a wealthy suburb of San Francisco. Mr. and Mrs. Morgan and their five children lived in a large, three-story, fashionable Victorian house with servants. During this era in America (the beginning of the Gilded Age) members of the lower classes couldn't attend public school, and even in the wealthiest of families, girls were not encouraged to attend high school. But Mr. and Mrs. Morgan strongly believed that a good education was important for all five of their children.

In 1867, Charles Morgan had sailed to California as he followed the flock of fortune seekers of the 1849 gold rush. After he married Eliza Parmelee, daughter of a self-made millionaire from the East Coast, Charles lured Eliza to California with stories of riches to be found. Eliza's parents couldn't sway their strong-willed daughter from traveling west with her new husband.

Though Charles Morgan was unlucky in his many failed investments and get-rich-quick schemes, Julia loved her father's happy-go-lucky spirit. Fortunately, the Morgan family was able to enjoy an upscale lifestyle with the assistance from Eliza's family money. Eliza's parents paid for their home, and several East Coast visits for Eliza and the children.

On one visit to New York City when Julia was six years old, she became ill with scarlet fever. She was bedridden for several weeks and suffered multiple ear infections. Worried for Julia's health, Mrs. Morgan overly protected the frail child and tried to have her stay close to home and rest. The strong-willed Julia rebelled, wanting to do the same activities as her brothers, such as playing on their gym equipment and archery. In her travels to the East Coast, Julia loved visits with her cousin Lucy, who was married to Pierre LeBrun, a very successful architect with a well-known firm in New York City. Through Lucy's husband, Julia learned about the architecture field, and LeBrun mentored her in her career path.

In high school, Julia's favorite classes were advanced math, physics, Latin, and German. She liked doing homework rather than going out with friends or to parties. When it was time to plan Julia's debutante party, she was not interested. In the 1890s, debutante balls or coming-out parties signaled to society that young ladies were ready to meet young men and get married. Julia explained to her mom that she wasn't interested in marriage; her loves were school and studying, especially complicated math problems. Besides, Julia didn't like parties. She wanted a career—in music or medicine, she wasn't sure. More women were studying in colleges, and she was determined to have an occupation. Mrs. Morgan realized that Julia's strong will would help her to do anything she set her mind to. Julia's sister, Emma, was just as determined and went to college and earned a law degree. Meanwhile, their brothers, Parmelee, Avery, and Sam, were average students who didn't share their sisters' ambitions.

In 1890, Julia enrolled in the University of California at Berkeley, near her Oakland home. Julia's brother Avery had to escort her to classes—a requirement that her parents demanded because a young woman traveling alone was socially unacceptable at the time. As the only girl in her math and science classes, she was not welcomed by her male classmates. Girls were not supposed to do well in or even like math and science, but Julia loved those classes, so she learned to ignore the harsh treatment and excel nonetheless.

As her college studies continued, Julia decided she wanted to become an architect. She was impressed with the projects her cousin's husband, Pierre LeBrun, had designed. More so, she was interested in learning how things worked—studying electricity, heat, magnetism, mechanics, and sound. She equated architecture with solving a complex math problem or composing a symphony, and she loved working on projects step-by-step.

Architecture was not a degree program offered at the university at that time. The closest program was in civil engineering, which focuses on building materials and structural stress. Accordingly, Julia became the only woman to receive an engineering degree at the University of California in 1894.

One of Julia's mentors at the university was Bernard Maybeck, an architect who taught geometry at the school and architecture in his home. Julia loved his design philosophies: he believed a house grows out of the land, a house works with the owner, and a house should inspire. To become an architect, Julia would have to get a degree in architecture, and Maybeck believed that Julia should study architecture in the best school in the world—in Paris at École des Beaux-Arts (the School of Fine Arts). It had been a strictly all-male school for more than 250 years, though it was rumored that they might start admitting female students. Julia was up for the challenge.

Once in Paris, Julia Morgan discovered that not only did the Beaux-Arts deny women entry to the school,

> Everywhere Julia went, she took her sketchpad and pencil and recorded every interesting detail.

but it also restricted the number of foreigners who could enroll. Still, Julia was determined to apply. She began to study French and worked in an architect's studio, called an atelier. Julia was the only woman working in the office, and she felt lonely when she was left out of the young men's pranks and jokes. She was also running out of money, though she refused all offers of financial help. She felt that the pressures of "homesickness and nervous strain of exams" were more of a burden. Even though Julia missed home, she loved Paris and explored the many things to see, while recording every interesting detail in her sketchpad.

The Beaux-Arts finally allowed women to take entrance exams in 1897. Julia had a difficult time with the math portion because the metric system was used in Europe, but not America at that time. She placed 42nd out of 376 applicants—but the school only took the top 30. She took the exam again six months later, but the judges purposely took extra points off her test score so she would not be admitted. In a letter to her cousin Lucy and Pierre LeBrun, she shared that the jury explained "'*ne voudraient pas encouragé [sic] les jeunes filles*'" ("they do not want to encourage young girls"), and she decided to try again, "just to show '*les jeunes filles*' (young girls) are not discouraged." Another six months later, a determined Julia took the exam again and passed, placing 13th. She later admitted to her parents the secret to her passing: during the oral portion of the exam, even the strongest of men caved under the pressure—they would "get up, tremble, turn white, clutch their hands and seem to have no power left." Julia said that she was surprised by her strength in handling the pressure while speaking in front of the board; but, of course, she now had the honor of being the first woman admitted to the prestigious school.

The next challenge was that the Beaux-Arts did not award a certificate to students over 30. Julia completed the program in two years, a month before her 30th birthday, sealing the deal with a first-prize win in the student architecture competition. Julia was now the first woman to be granted the École de Beaux-Arts certificate.

Julia continued to work in Paris and New York, but she was anxious to return to California, so she turned down several job offers. Eventually, John Galen Howard, another École graduate, hired Julia to help him work on the University of California's building program—a gift from Phoebe Hearst, the widow of a multimillionaire. Julia and Mrs. Hearst knew each other from when Julia was a student at the university. Mrs. Hearst supported women and their ambitions, and she was one of the many benefactors who had offered to help Julia financially at the École de Beaux-Arts but whom Julia turned down.

Julia's projects were starting to attract attention. She designed the outdoor Greek Theatre for the university and a bell tower for Mills College, a women's college in nearby Oakland, CA. Both were constructed of reinforced concrete—a new technique used in England and France, but not yet in America. As an employee of Howard's, Julia also designed a permanent home remodeled from a hunting lodge for Mrs. Hearst, who personally requested Julia as architect. Her estate, Hacienda del Pozo de Verona, when finished, had 92 rooms, with a bowling alley, banquet room, swimming pool, and ballroom. Mrs. Hearst's only child, William Randolph Hearst, met Julia when he visited his mother, and found they shared a love of architecture and the California landscape.

While Julia worked for Howard, she worked out of her parents' garage, which she had turned into a studio. She had always dreamed of heading her own studio. When Julia heard the gossip that Howard raved about his wonderful designer and added, "to whom I have to pay almost nothing, as it is a woman," she decided to take action. To work independently, architects need to be licensed by the state in which they work. In 1904, Julia passed the California state exam, became the first licensed architect in the state, and opened her own office in San Francisco.

But in April 1906, Julia's world came tumbling down. Her entire office—including all her drawings, records, and office equipment—was destroyed in the San Francisco earthquake. Fires raged for days, and firefighters had no means to stop the blazes. The massive quake left 700 people dead, 300,000 people homeless, and 28,000 buildings collapsed. Some of the few buildings that survived were Julia's designs using reinforced concrete—her bell tower and library at Mills College and her University of California buildings. People quickly started talking about her because most of San Francisco had to be rebuilt to withstand the possibility of another earthquake, and she was the only architect in America with this expertise.

The highly anticipated Fairmont Hotel had survived the quake but was left an empty shell by the fire that raged through it 24 hours later. The owners, anxious to rebuild, approached Julia for the project with the stipulation that they needed the Fairmont ready within a year for their grand celebration. Julia was up for the challenge. She worked closely on every step of the project and gained a reputation for high quality and professionalism—from climbing up high ladders in her tailored suit to ripping out substandard tile work with her hands. On the one-year anniversary of the Great Earthquake, the Fairmont Hotel opened on time for a grand celebration announcing the rebirth of San Francisco, and the hotel remained the city's social center, providing housing for the city's wealthy.

With her success from the Fairmont Hotel commission, Julia was the talk of the town—a double-edged sword. The fame brought her endless clients, but she was reserved and shunned attention. After talking to one reporter, she vowed never again to be interviewed. Instead, Julia devoted herself to the passion of her design work. Often referred to as "the client's architect," she insisted on working on a design or project with the owner, family, or occupants of the building.

On building sites, the petite Julia Morgan, called J.M. or Miss Morgan, would stand out in a sea of workmen. At only five feet tall she may have seemed fragile, but she was strong. She wore wire-rimmed glasses, with her hair pulled back in a bun. She thought nothing of crawling up a ladder or scaffolding to check construction of a building in a tailored suit and silk blouse. On one construction site, she fell off the scaffolding and plunged down three or four floors into the Sacramento River. After the men on the job site pulled her out of the water, she insisted on going back up on the scaffolding.

Julia refused to carry a purse, so her pockets were usually full of pencils, pens, and sketchpads. She constantly had an envelope on hand to draw a plan or write notes. She was forever on the go, and coworkers jokingly said that she lived on coffee and chocolate. She never attended social gatherings or attracted attention to herself, nor entered competitions, wrote articles, spoke at conferences, or wrote any sort of memoir.

Though she broke through the men-only barriers of the architecture world, Julia Morgan didn't consider herself a woman's suffragist. Many of her clients were independently wealthy women with their own homes and projects. Most notably, Julia's longtime client Phoebe Hearst was a supporter of the YWCA, an organization growing in California that supported independent women. Mrs. Hearst recommended to the board that Julia design all the YMCA locations, as well as the YMCA conference center named Asilomar, on 30 acres of land on the California coastline that Mrs. Hearst had donated.

In 1919, Phoebe Hearst passed away, and her son came back to California for the funeral. One day, while he was in town, William Randolph Hearst walked into Julia Morgan's office and, true to his word, told Julia that he had a project for her. He said, "Miss Morgan, we are tired of camping out and want something more comfortable on the hill."

The hill that Hearst was referring to was 250,000 acres of undeveloped land located in San Simeon, California, along the coast between Los Angeles and San Francisco. William Randolph Hearst's father had bought the land in 1865, and it had

Hearst Castle, San Simeon, California.
Courtesy Hearst Castle®/California State Parks

been the site of many Hearst family camping trips. With his mother's passing, William Randolph inherited the land. At first, Hearst wanted a bungalow, but the project soon turned into "the ranch." Hearst called it "the Enchanted Hill."

Julia Morgan traveled from San Francisco to San Simeon to work on design and construction for "the ranch" from 1919 to 1938, almost 30 years. She would work on her many other projects from her San Francisco office during the week, then take a train and taxi ride during the night, arrive in the morning to work on "the ranch," and then turn around and work another week in San Francisco. The scope of the project grew over the years. As Hearst's wealth steadily increased, the project changed from a bungalow for his family to a museum for his amazing art collection from around the world to, ultimately, a castle for entertaining guests from the social elite.

First, Julia had to create a five-mile winding road just to get to the building site. Housing for all the crew had to be built. A wharf had to be built for all the building supplies shipped in from San Francisco, as well as delivery of Hearst's art treasures. Miss Morgan designed an aqueduct system to pipe mountain spring water in from five miles away, and tons of earth had to be trucked up the hill from below to create the lush landscaping designs that Hearst wanted.

The building projects started with three guest cottages, which became mansions with 10 to 18 rooms each. The grounds covered 127 acres and included the Neptune pool built around the front of an ancient Roman temple with columns and statues. Hearst started collecting animals as well as ancient art. The zoo that Miss Morgan designed was once the largest private zoo in the world.

In the 1930s and 1940s, the ranch was the social center for the rich and famous. Guests included President Calvin Coolidge, British Prime Minister Winston Churchill, silent film actor Charlie Chaplin, actor Clark Gable, aviator Amelia Earhart, and filmmaker

Julia Morgan and William Randolph Hearst.
Courtesy of Hearst Castle®/ California State Parks

MARION MANLEY,
"THE WOMAN WHO BUILT MIAMI"

In the early 20th century, while Julia Morgan was working as an architect in San Francisco, Marion Manley was building Miami. In 1917, after graduating from the University of Illinois with a bachelor of science degree in architecture, Marion moved to Florida. Her brother, who had just won the commission to pave the main street in Miami, saw the opportunities for architects there. Marion quickly became a registered architect in the state and opened her own office in 1924. In her 60-year career, she designed more 100 residences and commercial buildings and was mostly known for her buildings at the University of Miami campus. Surprisingly, she had no relatives in architecture or role models, and never stepped into an architecture studio until her senior year in college. Years later, she explained to a reporter, "I wanted to work at something in which I used my brain and my hands."

Howard Hughes. Miss Morgan stayed out of the public eye but could be seen occasionally with Hearst, huddled together over drawings and discussing plans for the ranch. Today, Hearst's ranch is known as Hearst Castle, though Hearst didn't like guests calling it a castle since he already had an ancient stone castle in Wales.

Julia Morgan is frequently quoted as saying, "Never turn down a job because you think it's too small; you don't know where it can lead." True to this maxim, Julia Morgan designed a total of more than 700 structures. Her house designs, from small bungalows to huge mansions, all met the needs of the owners, including little details for the children such as secret hiding places or outdoor play areas. Her school layouts were designed around outdoor play areas, incorporating her childhood love of the outdoors. She designed churches, stores, hospitals, swimming pools, women's clubs, crematoriums, and college campuses—all bearing her signature stamp but not defined by a single Julia Morgan style. The clients' needs were always at the forefront of her designs. In 1950, the same year that William Randolph Hearst passed away, Julia closed her architectural design office, at the age of 79. True to her private nature, she instructed her staff to burn any documents or drawings that her clients didn't want. She explained, "My buildings will be my legacy. . . . They will speak for me long after I'm gone."

"My buildings will be my legacy. . . . They will speak for me long after I'm gone."

Always on the go—both mentally and physically— Julia traveled alone around the world in her later years. She finally put away her passport and returned to San Francisco, where she died on February 2, 1957, at the age of 85.

LEARN MORE

Julia Morgan (Women of Achievement) by Cary James and Matina S. Horner (Chelsea House Publications, 1990)

Julia Morgan, Architect of Dreams by Ginger Wadsworth (Lerner Publications, 1990)

Julia Morgan Built a Castle by Celeste Mannis and Miles Hyman (Viking, 2006)

MARION MAHONY GRIFFIN

Frank's Right-Hand Man

A member of famous Prairie School architect Frank Lloyd Wright's studio once said of his colleague Marion Mahony, "She was the most talented member of Frank Lloyd Wright's staff. . . . Mr. Wright would occasionally sit at Marion's board and work on her drawings. I recall one hilarious occasion when his work ruined the drawing. On that occasion Andrew Willatzen, an outspoken member of the staff, loudly proclaimed that Marion Mahony was Wright's superior as a draftsman. As a matter of fact, she was. Wright took the statement of her superiority equably."

Marion Lucy Mahony was born on February 14, 1871, in Chicago, Illinois, to Jeremiah and Clara Hamilton Mahony. Her father was an Irish poet, journalist, and educator, and her mother was a teacher. Just months after Marion's birth, her parents left the city. They carried the infant Marion in a clothesbasket with her older brother, Jerome, and moved to Winnetka, a then-rural suburb of Chicago. Marion grew up appreciating nature. About the area that she lived in, called Hubbard Woods, she wrote:

In the loveliest spot you can imagine, beyond suburbia—four houses and no others within a mile in any direction. Our home was at the head of a lovely ravine. A half mile walk through the beautiful forest to the east took us to the shores of Lake Michigan with bluffs 50 feet high and a wide sandy beach, to the west, half a mile through scrub to the marvelous Skokie, headwaters of the Chicago River, stretching for endless miles.

When city guests would come to their Winnetka home, nine-year-old Marion was asked to perform her tree-climbing feats. The guests would gather on the veranda and watch barefooted Marion climb like a monkey all the way up the tree just in front of the house. The branches went well above the top of the two-story house. The guests would tease the boys because they couldn't do it.

After 10 years in the suburbs, the family's house burned to the ground, and they moved back to the city. Marion's father found employment as a school principal, but he died when Marion was 12. Her mother raised Marion and her four siblings, and herself soon got a job as principal at Komensky School, in a poor neighborhood of Chicago. Marion's grandmother and Aunt Myra moved into the house to help.

Marion and her siblings were a rambunctious bunch. Marion explained, "When the five [Jerome, Marion, Gerald, Georgine, Leslie] were through the teachers said, 'Thank God that's the last of the Mahonys.'" Marion graduated from West Division High School in 1890.

With financial assistance from a local civic leader, Mary Wilmarth, Marion left Chicago in 1892 to study architecture at MIT in Boston. She had classes in languages, political history, political economy, anthropology, and literature, in addition to her architecture classes. She also became interested in theater and was in several college plays. Her thesis title was "House and Studio for a Painter." Unsure about her abilities as an architect, she wrote that she "rebelled and told the head of the Architecture Department I couldn't do that sort of thing, that perhaps I wasn't an architect. He said well wasn't there something I would be interested to do. And I said well domestic work was the only thing that appealed to me, and he said well do the home of an architect but doll it up a bit. So I did."

In 1894, Marion was the second woman to graduate from MIT with a bachelor of science degree in architecture. With her degree in hand, Marion returned home to Chicago. Her first job was as a drafter with her cousin, Dwight Perkins, who had grown up with her family and was nicknamed "the sixth Mahony." The next year, she started working for Frank Lloyd Wright in his studio in Oak Park, Illinois. In 1898, Marion took the new Illinois architects' licensing exam and passed, making her the first licensed female architect in America.

Frank Lloyd Wright's son John wrote about the draftsmen in his autobiography, *My Father, Frank Lloyd Wright,* "Five men, two women. They wore flowing ties and smocks suitable to the realm. . . . They worshiped Papa! Papa liked them! I know now that each one of them was then making valuable contributions to the pioneering of the modern American architecture for which my father gets the full glory, headaches, and recognition today!"

Frank Lloyd Wright was the leader of the Prairie style that revolutionized architecture in the early 1900s. Unlike Marion, Wright wasn't a registered architect; he took only two civil engineering classes and may not have even graduated from high school. Marion's unique style of drawing, incorporating nature with a Japanese feel, had a more illustrative quality than the norm at the time. The beautiful drawings sold the designs to Wright's clients. Marion has been called one of the greatest delineators of all time for her drawings and sketches. Wright's son John said of Marion, "She was so ugly and her laugh was so boisterous that I was afraid of her. Later, after seeing and appreciating her beautiful drawings, I thought her beautiful."

In September 1909, when Wright dashed off to Europe with his client and neighbor's wife, Mamah Cheney, he left his office in the hands of Herman Von Holst. The only stipulation that Herman had in taking over the firm was that Marion join him. He recalled later, "I had engaged Miss Mahony to work in my office, as I could not carry on Wright's work without her help." Marion insisted on being allowed to organize and direct her own studio to do the work. When the news broke in the States that Wright was in fact living with Mamah Cheney in Berlin, the *Chicago Tribune* headline read,

> "[Marion] was so ugly and her laugh was so boisterous that I was afraid of her. Later, after seeing and appreciating her beautiful drawings, I thought her beautiful."

LEAVE FAMILIES, ELOPE TO EUROPE. Marion had become good friends with Catherine, Wright's wife, while working at the Oak Park studio, and spent a lot of time consoling her friend.

Marion worked on several commissions outside of Wright's office. In 1903, she designed All Souls Church in Evanston, Illinois, for her friend and minister, Reverend James Vilas Blake. She also designed three homes in Decatur, Illinois, for Robert and Adolph Mueller and E. P. Irving and a home in Grand Rapids, Michigan, for David Amberg. While von Holst was in charge of the office, Marion designed lavish homes for Henry Ford and Childe Harold Wills, designer of the Model T. Though neither were built, they would have been iconic landmarks to rival Wright's homes. In 1910, Marion's drawings of Wright's designs filled about half of what came to be known as the Wasmuth Portfolio, a collection that established Wright as an architectural genius.

HARRIET MORRISON IRWIN

While Marion Mahony Griffin was known for her unique and beautiful design drawings, the first woman to patent a building plan was Harriet Irwin. With nine children underfoot, she studied architecture on her own and felt that her position as a housewife taught her to understand what was needed in house design. Her 1869 patent was titled "Improvement in the Construction of Houses" and incorporated interconnected hexagons making a large hexagon-shaped house. Her design created more space using fewer materials and was more efficient in ventilating and lighting. From her unique view as a housewife, it eliminated sharp corners, making it easier to clean.

Another employee at the Wright studio was Walter Burley Griffin. Walter had graduated with an architectural degree from University of Illinois in 1899 and started working at Wright's studio in 1901 after he passed the state licensing exam. He had a love for gardens, and he landscaped most of Wright's houses—though he left the studio in 1906 after he quarreled with Wright. After Wright left for Europe, Marion convinced Herman to hire Walter back on.

Marion and Walter began spending time together and soon became a couple. They spent their weekends together canoeing the rivers of northeastern Illinois and northwestern Indiana. In a canoe they named *Allana*, they paddled up the Des Plaines River, down the Fox River, even passing Starved Rock on the Illinois River—the one-day trip was 45 miles.

Marion later recounted the story of their relationship in her memoirs. She romanticized their courtship, portraying Walter as Socrates and herself as his wife Xanthippe. In *The Magic of America*, she wrote, "Back to the office and the drafting board; and pleasant work . . . but somehow the work of that 'pink-haired' (so called by my 5 year old niece) blond of a Socrates was gradually capturing her imagination."

Marion and Walter married in June 1911. Marion wrote, "When I encountered Walter Burley Griffin I was first swept off my feet by my delight in his achievements in my profession, then through a common bond of interests in nature and intellectual pursuits and then with the man himself. It was by no means a case of love at first sight but it was a madness when it struck."

For 10 years, Walter had been waiting for the announcement of an international competition to design Canberra, a new capital city in Australia. In April 1911, he finally heard the news, and in May he received the requirements. Walter set up a studio in his parents' home in Elmhurst, Illinois. The deadline was January 1912; that didn't leave much time for the designs! In October, Marion lectured Walter, "For the love of Mike when are you going to get started on those Capital plans? How much time do you think there is left anyway? . . . Perhaps you can design a city in two days but the drawings take time and that falls on me. . . . Perhaps I am the swiftest draftsman in town but I can't do the impossible. What's the use of thinking about a thing like this for ten years if when the time comes you don't get it done in time!"

With the help of several architect friends, as well as Marion's sister Gertrude and her fiancée, they finished the plans on New Year's Eve. They put the huge crate of drawings on the last boat to Australia to get it there on time.

In May 1912, Walter won the international competition to design the new city of Australia, Canberra, partly on the strength of Mahony's renderings. In May 1914, Marion and Walter departed Chicago for Australia, making their new home in Melbourne. Walter worked on Canberra until 1920, and then the couple decided to stay in Australia permanently. They moved to Walter's planned suburb, Castlecrag, north of Sydney.

Marion designed only one building in Australia under her own name. Her involvement in her husband's office varied through the years, but in general she devoted more and more time to artistic and social causes.

Marion and Walter returned to the United States several times, in 1925 and again in 1932. Marion designed a mural for Chicago's George Armstrong Public School.

In 1935, Walter designed the library for the University of Lucknow in India. Marion joined her husband there in June 1936. She managed the office, made working drawings, and drew watercolor perspectives of Walter's final buildings. Once

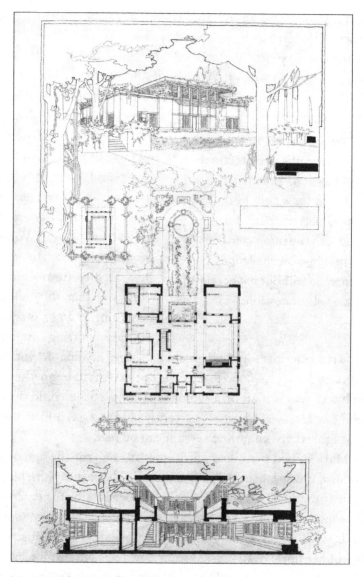

Marion Mahony Griffin rendered (drew) this plan of the F. P. Marshall Dwelling, Winnetka, Illinois, 1910 (not built), designed by her husband, Walter Burley Griffin.
Courtesy of the Mary and Leigh Block Museum of Art, Northwestern University, Gift of Marion Mahony Griffin, 1985.1.100

again, she created a rendering style that matched the magnificence of the architecture it portrayed.

In February 1937, Walter died. Marion closed the India office and returned to Australia, but by the following year was back in Illinois. In the last years of her life, Marion wrote *The Magic in America*, a memoir of more than 1,400 pages and with 650 illustrations, and encouraged other women to enter the industry, writing, "Women should continue to enter the architectural profession, and that they should be willing to do so as equals of men, putting up with the same sacrifices and physical challenges as men do without expecting special concessions. It doesn't matter whether an architect was a man or a woman, as long as she could do the job." *The Magic in America* is currently held at the Art Institute of Chicago, where an online version can be read.

> "Women should continue to enter the architectural profession, and that they should be willing to do so as equals of men, putting up with the same sacrifices and physical challenges as men do without expecting special concessions."

Marion died penniless on August 10, 1961, at the age of 90. Because it was labeled a "pauper's death," her ashes were placed in an unmarked grave. In 1997, with the permission of her family, her ashes were moved to Chicago's architects' cemetery, Graceland. With a new granite marker embossed with the image of one of her floral drawings, Marion now rests with other leaders of architecture, such as Daniel Burnham, Louis Sullivan, John Root, and Ludwig Mies van der Rohe.

LEARN MORE

100 Women Architects in the Studio of Frank Lloyd Wright: Volume 1 (Beverly Willis Architecture Foundation, 2009)

The Magic of America electronic edition by Marion Mahony Griffin www.artic.edu/magicofamerica

Marion Mahony Reconsidered by David Van Zanten (University of Chicago Press, 2011)

NORMA MERRICK SKLAREK

The Rosa Parks of Architecture

When Norma Merrick Sklarek became the first black woman to be made a fellow of the prestigious American Institute of Architects in 1980 for her extraordinary contributions in the field, she quipped of the title, "It's a sexist title, but I'll take it."

Norma Merrick was born in Harlem on April 15, 1926. Her parents were both from islands in the West Indies; Walter was from St. Vincent and Amelia from Barbados. When Norma was a small child, her father became a physician, graduating from Howard University in Washington, DC, in 1935. Her mother was one of 10 children and was a seamstress in a factory.

An only child, Norma received extra attention and encouragement from her parents. She said, "Although both my parents

Norma Merrick Sklarek.
Used by permission of Norma Sklarek Family Archives, © 2012

adored me, I did lots of things with my father that ordinary girls did not do—like going fishing, painting the house, and doing carpentry work." Born right before the Great Depression, Norma had to learn how to help with many things around the house and became very self-sufficient. She always kept her hands busy, and she drew portraits for relatives, decorated rooms, painted murals, and refinished furniture. When Norma got her first $10, instead of buying a doll or a toy, she bought a how-to book about drawing.

Norma went to Catholic school in Harlem from first to sixth grade, but she wanted very much to attend a public junior high school. Her parents transferred her to an all-girls school and gave the school officials a false address to get her in because they lived in the wrong neighborhood. Hunter High School was a mile and a half away, so her parents gave her a nickel for subway fare. Norma would walk and save the nickel for an ice cream cone on the way back home.

Norma's new school was about 98 percent white, and Norma was made to feel inferior by the other students as well as her teachers. She excelled in school, even in classes she didn't like, just to prove herself. With her high grades, she had the freedom to pursue any profession, and was interested in art, science, and math. She thought about a career in physics. The typical female jobs at the time, like teaching and nursing, did not appeal to her. One day, Norma's father asked her, "What about architecture?" He thought that would be more exciting for her. Norma knew nothing about architecture, but it did combine all her interests, so she took her father's suggestion.

Norma took one year of classes at Barnard College in New York City to prepare herself for the demanding architecture program at Columbia University. That first year at college was difficult because it was so different from high school, and she

worked extremely hard just to pass her classes. She spent the
summer thinking about transferring to another college. Norma's parents let her decide what to do. Their only requirement
was that she must attend a college near home. For the social
benefits, she wanted to go away to her father's college, Howard
University, an all-black school. This one time, her father said no.

With a strict quota system for admitting women at Columbia, Norma applied and was accepted based on her science background and high grades. Norma explained her experience:

> Other colleges at Columbia may have had similar gender
> and racial quotas, but it was quite obvious in architecture.
> The school didn't want to waste space on women. They
> felt that women would get married and return home
> to have children. The competition was fierce. I entered
> with a minimum requirement of one year of liberal arts,
> whereas many of my male classmates had bachelor's or
> master's degrees. Some of the students were World War
> II veterans receiving financial aid from the G. I. Bill.
> Other students had work experience as draftsmen. I was
> the youngest in class, competing with mature, experi-
> enced men.

In 1950, Norma and one other woman graduated with a
degree in architecture from Columbia. Then, she started the
task of looking for a job. After being turned down by 19 architectural firms in private practice, she was finally hired by the City of
New York. Norma felt uncertain about why she had been turned
down so many times. Was it because she was black? A young
woman? Or could it be because of the recession at the time?

At the civil-service job, the work she did was uncreative.
She realized that she really wanted to work in private practice,

but to do so meant that she needed to be a registered architect. Norma stayed at the city job for three years to meet the requirements needed to take the test, and then passed the four-day exam, shocking many people. The dean of the school told her that not even some straight-A students had passed the exam on their first try. In 1954, she became the first African American woman architect to be licensed in the state of New York.

After Norma passed the licensing exam she left her job with the city. Then, married and expecting her second child, she found a position with a small firm where most of her work was designing bathrooms in buildings. It was unglamorous work, but it would prove a stepping stone. In 1955, she was hired by one of the largest firms in the country: Skidmore, Owings & Merrill (SOM). Wanting more challenging work, she let her supervisor know that she was willing to do any projects placed in front of her. He soon realized that Norma could get any job done. In fact, one day he apologized to her for giving her all the projects with the tight deadlines, but, he explained, she was the only person that he could depend on to get the job done on time.

Norma had been unaware that she was getting the toughest projects. She quickly gained the respect of veteran architects, who started coming to her for help in solving their design problems. While working at SOM, Norma said she didn't feel that she was discriminated against because of her sex or race. She was just too busy to even notice. She worked at SOM for five years and during that time also taught architecture at City College in New York City two nights a week, all while raising her two sons. About this time, her first marriage ended, but Norma was able to maintain a normal schedule with the help of her mother and aunts.

In 1960, with the encouragement of friends, Norma moved to Los Angeles and started looking for work. Staff at one company told her that they had only hired women as secretaries or decorators, but they could try something new and hire her. She chose instead to work for another large, well-known architecture firm, Gruen Associates, and got her California state license in 1962. With that, she became the first black woman registered architect in California.

After she had been working at Gruen for several years, Norma heard that the firm had a policy at the time she was hired to not employ black people. When she asked the architect who had hired her about this policy, he looked her straight in the face and said, "That's true." Yet, Norma worked at Gruen for 20 years and became the head of the architecture department, supervising a team of architects.

BEVERLY L. GREENE, FIRST AFRICAN AMERICAN ARCHITECT

In 1942, Beverly Greene was the first black woman registered as a licensed architect in the United States. The only child of a lawyer and a homemaker, she grew up in Chicago and earned a bachelor of science degree in architectural engineering from the University of Illinois in 1936 and a master's in city planning in 1937. While working in New York City, Greene worried that she would not be able to work on Stuyvesant Town, New York City, a private housing project. She read that Stuyvesant was "not allowing Negroes to live in the development." She was eventually hired to work on the development. Greene was also the first woman and first African American hired by the Chicago Housing Authority.

Pacific Design Center,
Los Angeles, called
"the Blue Whale."
Library of Congress,
LC-HS503-523

Gruen's design work was comprised of mainly malls and shopping plazas, which gained founder Victor Gruen the nickname "Father of the Shopping Mall." Norma worked on the Santa Monica Mall and Place, Fox Plaza in San Francisco, South Coast Plaza in Orange County, and many others. Among Norma's high-profile projects were the American embassy in Tokyo and Pacific Design Center in Los Angeles.

While working at Gruen, she was asked to teach architecture at the University of California in Los Angeles, where she taught for six years. She also coached students for many years for the licensing exam, even inviting them to her house to study.

In 1980, feeling that she needed a change, Norma left Gruen and started working for Welton Becket and Associates (WBA). Her first project at WBA was for Terminal One at the

Los Angeles International Airport. The project had very strict deadlines due to the upcoming 1984 Summer Olympics in L.A. Norma's design had to safely move people in and out of the terminal. She was the only architect in the office who met her deadlines that year.

After working at WBA for five years, Norma cofounded what was at the time the largest architectural firm in the United States owned by women, called Siegel, Sklarek, Diamond (SSD). After a few years, fueled by an argument with one of her partners, Norma decided to leave SSD to pursue larger and more profitable projects. She was immediately asked by Jon Jerde to become a principal at his firm, Jerde Associates, an internationally renowned architectural firm.

> "I believe that a professional woman needs a partner who is understanding of her needs. The male ego sometimes is very delicate."

Norma had married Rolf Sklarek, an architect who studied in Germany at the Bauhaus school and also worked with Norma at Gruen in 1967. Rolf passed away in 1984, and Norma married Cornelius Welch, a physician, the following year. Speaking about the challenges of combining marriage and a career,

AFRICAN AMERICAN ARCHITECTS

Today, about 274 female African Americans are registered architects in the United States, out of approximately 120,000 licensed architects and 1,814 African American registered architects total.

Norma said, "I believe that a professional woman needs a partner who is understanding of her needs. The male ego sometimes is very delicate. It very often cannot deal with a wife who may be more successful that he. . . . Both Rolf and Cornelius possessed secure egos, and were able to accept my success because of their own success."

When Norma retired in the late 1990s, she traveled, played golf, and gave lectures on architecture. Every spring she hosted a garden party at her house to celebrate the blossoming of her 200 epiphyllum orchids. Norma passed away on February 2, 2012, at the age of 85. For the memorial, her husband Cornelius held the last epiphyllum party in her honor.

LEARN MORE

I Dream a World: Portraits of Black Women Who Changed America by Brian Lanker and Barbara Summers (Stewart, Tabori & Chang, 1989)

No Mountain High Enough: Secrets of Successful African American Women by Dorothy Ehrhart-Morrison (Conari Press, 1997)

Women Trailblazers of California: Pioneers to the Present by Gloria G. Harris and Hannah S. Cohen (History Press, 2012)

DENISE SCOTT BROWN

Husband-and-Wife Design Team

D enise Scott Brown, one of the world's foremost women architects, was born to Phyllis Hepker, a free spirit who spent her childhood in the African wilderness.

Phyllis and her brothers were homeschooled by a governess. They read stories, learned natural history and care of animals in the veld (African grassland) and on the farm, and made musical instruments and toys from materials at hand around them. Later, when the teenage Phyllis went to boarding school, she found sympathetic teachers who allowed her to do her homework, as she was accustomed, up a tree.

Phyllis entered architecture school in South Africa in 1928, but she returned home to Zambia after two years to help her

Denise Scott Brown, 1967.
Courtesy of VSBA

parents run the family hotel. Phyllis's parents—originally Jewish emigrants from Latvia—settled in Zambia at the turn of the 20th century when it was still lion country. While working at the hotel, Phyllis met and married Shim Lakofski, a young South African of Lithuanian Jewish origin, and they made a home in the mining town of Nkana. Phyllis gave birth to Denise on October 3, 1931. But when Denise fell ill, possibly with malaria, the couple decided to raise their family in Johannesburg.

The family eventually grew to include two sisters and a brother for Denise. Phyllis shared her passions for reading, nature, and "making things" (including traps for anteaters), with her children. She also imparted her enthusiasm for modern architecture and her love of the flat-roofed house with big windows that was designed for her family by three of her former architecture classmates.

At four years old, Denise knew she wanted to be an architect like her mom. But at six, she changed her mind: her new aim was to teach children like her grade school teacher. Denise was not only the youngest and smallest in her class, but she was also marked as "clever," and was one of just a few Jewish children there. Despite feeling like an outsider, Denise took pleasure from working with her hands and learning in action at her elementary school. By age 12, English and art were her favorite subjects, and Denise considered pursuing a career in linguistics or writing. But a perceptive family friend suggested research might be a better career path for her, noting, "You ask so many questions."

In high school, Denise joined an archeological club and excavated for Stone Age implements. Here, adults opened her eyes to life beyond school, and when a member recommended she reconsider architecture, Denise returned to her mother's field. The decision, made "without too very much knowledge," has lasted a lifetime.

In 1948, Denise followed her mother into the University of the Witwatersrand, "Wits," in Johannesburg. But before starting architecture, she spent a year delving further into English, French, and psychology. In 1949, her first day in architecture brought a surprise: "There were all these men around, and I thought, 'What are they doing here?'" Denise had known only women architects and concluded that it was women's work. One of the men in her studio, Robert Scott Brown, would later become her husband.

> "There were all these men around, and I thought, 'What are they doing here?'"

The architecture program included a yearlong internship in an architect's office, and Denise decided to spend it overseas. In 1952, she began interning in London but in parallel took the entrance exam for a school there, the Architectural Association. When admitted, she transferred there. Although it meant two more years away from Robert, fate, she felt, was pushing her. After graduating, he joined her, and they married in London on July 21, 1955.

In South Africa, Denise had been drawn to African folk art that was influenced by Western culture, especially pop culture. When she and Robert traveled for their studies, they photographed architecture across Africa, Europe, the Middle East, and America. All the while, into their collection crept everyday objects and landscapes that testified to their growing fascination with pop culture. As postgraduates, their desire for travel grew more intense. Their 1955 honeymoon was a hitchhiking trip through Yugoslavia. In 1956, they crisscrossed France, Italy, Holland, and Germany, attended summer school in Venice, and worked in Rome for the architect Giuseppe Vaccaro. The couple camped, hiked, and traveled by cheap trains and old cars. For Denise, this was the best preparation possible for the global work she eventually undertook. And she still uses the photographs she took along the way.

Back in South Africa, the Scott Browns planned their further education. Where was the knowledge of urbanism—the way of life of city dwellers—to be found that they felt was needed to practice architecture and site planning in Africa? A respected London teacher recommended the University of Pennsylvania in Philadelphia, where architect Louis Kahn taught. So in 1958, they entered Penn's city planning school, just as the civil rights movement was bringing excitement and urgency to cities and intellectual ferment to Penn.

Robert and Denise were accustomed to learning during the tumult of South Africa under apartheid and Europe after World War II, but the American turmoil seemed familiar to them. Their travels had raised questions, particularly about urban life. They found that modernism was not addressing the needs of social life and urban blight / city decay. Now Penn offered the prospect of discovering methods to approach and reframe their questions. They spent a year in the most exciting intellectual environment they had known, while social unrest and burning issues heightened the quality of their educations.

Then, while on a Sunday drive in June 1959, a car in rural Pennsylvania ran a stop sign and hit the couple. Robert died in the ambulance.

Denise flew home, in deep sorrow for her personal loss but mourning, too, the tragedy of Robert's lost potential to help revitalize South Africa's architecture. But Denise overcame her devastation and returned to Penn in the fall, where she received her master's degree in city planning (1960) and architecture

(1965), and became a professor. She had also, without knowing it, left South Africa for good.

In 1960, Penn hired Denise to teach studio classes in urban design and city planning, which involved hands-on instruction with the students. Moving from student to teacher seemed a big step, but, she recalls, "If I had any pangs or stage fright, they didn't last more than 20 minutes. I realized that I was born to do this." The next year, courses in theory of architecture and planning were added to her duties.

Denise's new professorial role brought Robert Venturi into her life. In 1960, she and "Bob" met at a faculty meeting. When the idea of demolishing Frank Furness's Fine Arts Library was brought up, Denise protested that this would be "a huge mistake." She tells how, after the meeting, Robert came up and explained that he agreed with everything she said. Although happy to hear this, she replied, "Well, then, why didn't you say something?"

Denise Scott Brown and Robert Venturi in 1985.
Courtesy of VSBA

She and Bob formed a friendship based on shared enthusiasms in architecture. For several years they taught a course together and occasionally collaborated professionally. "When asked," Denise recalls, "I would go into Bob's office to give crits [critiques] of his architecture firm's work and he would visit my studio class in the evening to do the same." He would critique her students' work.

From 1960 to 1967, Denise taught at University of Pennsylvania; University of California, Berkeley; and University of California in Los Angeles (UCLA). Her focus was studio, the spine of architectural education, where students "make things" and "learn by doing"—where they design. To Denise, it was familiar territory, but she introduced innovations adapted from planning studios and added urban subject matter relating to popular culture, land economics, and social life. She believed the people and the atmosphere were important aspects of the architecture.

In 1966, having decided that her next studio would be centered on Las Vegas, Denise invited Bob to visit the city with her and to lecture at UCLA. Bob says, "First I fell in love with Las Vegas. Then I fell in love with Denise." They were married in Santa Monica, California, on July 23, 1967, and returned to Philadelphia where Denise joined Bob's firm. For the next 40 years they worked together.

Early on, Denise and Bob combined building their architecture practice and teaching. At Yale, their studios, including "Learning from Las Vegas" (1968) and "Learning from Levittown" (1971), employed both traditional architecture and planning studio methods, but their subject matter derived from the idea that "low art" sources—advertising signs, parking lots, roadside strips, and suburban tracts, the "urban sprawl" of the 1960s—could offer architects valuable lessons in design. Students pursued their ideas through architecture and its theories

ANNE TYNG

Another architectural partnership involved Anne Tyng and Louis Kahn. Anne, an architectural visionary, theorist, and teacher, was among the first women to receive a master's of architecture from Harvard University. Fascinated by complex shapes, Anne designed and developed the Tyng Toy, a set of interlocking plywood shapes that children could assemble and reassemble. In 1945, at age 25, she worked with Louis Kahn, and her geometric ideas were employed in the design of the Trenton Bath House and Yale University Art Gallery, among other projects. In 1953, Anne became pregnant with Kahn's child, and moved to Rome to avoid a scandal since he was a married man. In a letter to Kahn from Italy, Anne wrote, "I believe our creative work together deepened our relationship and the relationship enlarged our creativity. In our years of working together toward a goal outside ourselves, believing profoundly in each other's abilities helped us to believe in ourselves." The relationship ended in 1960 when he became involved with another woman. After 1968, Anne focused her attention on research, earning a doctoral degree from the University of Pennsylvania, where she taught for almost 30 years.

but turned as well to urban planning, media studies, pop art, and the social sciences.

In 1972, along with fellow architect Steven Izenour, Bob and Denise published *Learning from Las Vegas*, which is considered one of the most influential architectural theory books of the 20th century. The book has been read by generations of architects, and its content and methods remain models for architectural research and teaching. Over the decades, Bob and Denise

Denise Scott Brown in the Las Vegas desert, with the Strip in the background, 1966.
Courtesy of Robert Venturi

extended and developed the book's themes in their practice. Through their work, they crossed the world, covered wide terrains of thought regarding architecture, art, and social issues, and built many types of projects.

As principals of their firm, they led teams in the conceptual design, design development, and production of projects such as the Conseil Général Building in Toulouse, France, and the addition to the British National Gallery on Trafalgar Square in London. Denise is proud of her role as a designer on the office's major architectural projects, but she is also happy to have worked as an advocate planner for low-income communities threatened by an expressway in Philadelphia, and on plans and designs for the University of Pennsylvania, Dartmouth College, and the University of Michigan. Her work for these campuses involved first campus master and area planning and then design of important complexes within her plans: the Perelman Quadrangle at the University of Pennsylvania, Baker-Berry Library at Dartmouth, and the Palmer Drive Life Sciences Complex at the University of Michigan.

Denise has learned to stay involved down to the details of door hinges, to ensure that important projects' goals are maintained in the development of her designs. She loves to watch the completed buildings and open spaces in use and is delighted when people discover opportunities that she provided.

"It's like producing a jungle gym for grown-ups," she said. "We build it so that they can explore it, go where they want. Spaces can be used in many ways." Before one complex was completed, students discovered a shortcut across it that she had planned. She was thrilled when they broke down the construction fences to ride their bicycles along it. "There's nothing better," she said.

But Denise's life as a woman in architecture has been difficult. An article titled "Room at the Top? Sexism and the Star System in Architecture" recounts her early experience in the field:

The social trivia . . . "wives' dinners" . . . job interviews where the presence of the "architect's wife" distressed the board; dinners I must not attend because an influential member of the client group wants "the architect" as her date; Italian journalists who ignore Bob's request that they address me because I understand more Italian than he does; the tunnel vision of students toward Bob, the "so you're the architect!" to Bob, and the well-meant "so you're an architect too?" to me.

THE PRITZKER ARCHITECTURE PRIZE

Established in 1979 by the Pritzker family of Chicago through their Hyatt Foundation, this international prize is awarded each year to a living architect for contributions to humanity and the built environment through the art of architecture. Considered the Nobel Prize of architecture and the profession's highest honor, the honoree receives $100,000 and a bronze medallion.

In 1991, Bob received the Pritzker Prize for his body of architectural work, while Denise stayed home. It hurt them both that the committee didn't acknowledge their 25-year partnership. Bob has been vocal in objecting when she is omitted, and slowly Denise has found support and her own rewards.

"I have been helped," she said, "by noticing that the scholars whose work we most respect, the clients whose projects intrigue us, and the patrons whose friendship inspires us, have no problem in understanding my role. They are the sophisticates. Partly through them I gain heart and realize that, over the last 20 years, I have managed to do my work and, despite some sliding, to achieve my own self-respect."

Looking back on her aims and interests as a child, Denise found that during

"I've always had an oscillation between breadth and focus. And it's been a good one for me professionally, although it means it's very difficult to define me."

her career in architecture she had achieved most of them; in fact, "those things and a few more, because I had also become an urban planner. I had become very interested in the social sciences, as well. But they said to me at high school that my talents were very broad and I'd have to learn to focus. And the truth is, I've always had an oscillation between breadth and focus. And it's been a good one for me professionally, although it means it's very difficult to define me."

Robert announced his retirement in 2012, while Denise continues to lecture, write, and go into the office, still on Main Street in Manayunk, Philadelphia, about once a week.

LEARN MORE

Einstein's Wife: Work and Marriage in the Lives of Five Great Twentieth-Century Women by Andrea Gabor (Penguin, 1995)

Fuse: In, Re, De, Pro, Con (2012 video interview with Denise Scott Brown on her 81st birthday, in conversation with Amale Andraos, Columbia University Graduate School of Architecture, Planning, and Preservation, Felix Burrichter), www.youtube.com/watch?v=X_-6KKw0SUg

Having Words by Denise Scott Brown (Architectural Association Publications, 2009)

NATALIE de BLOIS

Builder of Buildings

N athaniel Owings, founder of the renowned architectural firm Skidmore, Owings & Merrill (SOM), praised Natalie de Blois in his autobiography, writing:

> Long, lean, quizzical, [Natalie] seemed fit to handle all comers. Handsome, her dark, straight eyes invited no nonsense. Her mind and hands worked marvels in design—and only she and God would ever know just how many great solutions, with the imprimatur of one of the male heroes of SOM, owed much more to her than was attributed either by SOM or the client.

Natalie de Blois, 1980s.
Courtesy of Natalie de Blois

Natalie Griffin was born on April 2, 1921, in Paterson, New Jersey. Her father, grandfather, and great-grandfather were all engineers. The Griffins were inventors of the Griffin Mill, machinery that aided in the development of Portland cement. Her mother was a schoolteacher. Money was tight during the Depression, but Natalie's mother and father encouraged all their five children to go to college. Her brother got a scholarship to a business school and her older sister got a scholarship to Vassar College. Of her four sisters and one brother, her parents thought that Natalie would be the child that would go into an artistic field. Natalie's father had hoped that one of his children would want to go into engineering. So when Natalie, at 10 years old, told her father that she wanted to be an architect, he was very encouraging.

In her 2004 interview for *The Oral History of Natalie de Blois*, Natalie said, "My father, being an engineer, had engineering tools, pencils, and scales, and proportional dividers, and different kinds of equipment around that I was familiar with. Drawing was something that I liked to do and so I'm sure it had a great deal to do with him possibly putting it in my head. But also I liked buildings, and houses, and plans."

> "My father, being an engineer, had engineering tools, pencils, and scales, and proportional dividers, and different kinds of equipment around that I was familiar with. Drawing was something that I liked to do."

The norm at the time was that girls took sewing and cooking classes in junior high school. Natalie's father went to the principal's office and insisted that Natalie be allowed to take mechanical drawing. She took the class with all boys.

When Natalie was 14, her interest in architecture was broadened on a field trip to New York City. She explained, "One of the first times that I really saw and appreciated architecture and what it did was when I saw a tenement exhibit that was in New York in 1937. . . . I went and saw this exhibit and was impressed by the whole field of housing."

At the 1939 New York World's Fair, Natalie's father was the civil engineer on the construction of the French pavilion and the Venezuelan building. He would come home every night and tell the family about the fair, throwing in a little of the French that he was trying to learn. When Natalie finally saw all the modern buildings at the fair, she was awestruck. Growing up in suburban Ridgewood, New Jersey, the kids would play in under-construction housing around the neighborhood, but Natalie had never been around so many large buildings and large construction projects.

Natalie wanted to go to college and study architecture, but architecture schools required that students attend an undergraduate program for two years before applying. Natalie's father wanted her to go to MIT, where he had graduated. But when she received a full scholarship to Western College for Women in Oxford, Ohio (now part of Miami University), she started there. The small school specialized in liberal arts, and Natalie enjoyed her classes in art, modern dance, and Latin.

Still, her father wanted her to go to architecture school, so he kept a watchful eye on the colleges. He discovered that Columbia University had just changed its rules and that students could apply to the architectural program with only one year of undergraduate study. When Natalie came home from college for the summer, she learned that her father had enrolled her at Columbia for the fall semester. It was 1940 and many male students were drafted into the military under the Selective Service and

Training Act signed by President Franklin D. Roosevelt to prepare the country for the impending Second World War. The college wanted more women to apply. There were 18 students in
the class; five of them were women.

A family friend contributed to Natalie's tuition, and she also
worked several jobs to help pay for college. Between 1940 and
1941, she taught drafting at Columbia to men who could then
use the skill to work for the airplane factories. She worked on
drawings of boilers for Babcock and Wilcox, who had contracts
with the Russian navy. She worked during the school year making drawings for Frederick Kiesler, an architect, theater set
designer, and professor. Kiesler took Natalie to the Guggenheim Museum's "Art of This Century" gallery and showed her
his universal chair design that was on exhibit. He couldn't draw
and wanted Natalie to create drawings for him.

In a 2004 interview for *SOM* magazine, Natalie explained
how she felt at Columbia: "I liked it. But already after my first
year I thought, Well, I want to get out of school and start working. . . . You're a woman and you're in a man's profession. You
better get a degree."

Her classes were math, descriptive geometry, statistics, introduction to design, and history. Every year she took classes in
materials and methods of construction, which were held in the
engineering building so they could actually test concrete and
steel. She took painting and sculpture too. She was so exhausted
from her heavy workload that when the professor would turn
off the lights to show slides for Natalie's history of architecture
classes, Natalie would fall asleep. Luckily, she had the history
book that the teacher was following, so she could study on her
own what she had missed.

Architecture students had required projects with limited
time to complete them, and every Saturday they had sketch

problems. Like at the French Beaux-Arts, design problems were presented in each drawing, and the students had to come up with an outline and develop a solution in one day. Drawing quickly was very important because students only had between 9:00 AM and 6:00 PM to finish the color and presentation.

In 1944, Natalie received her degree from the Columbia School of Architecture. Her thesis project was a design for a new community center for Ridgewood, New Jersey, her hometown. At graduation, she won two awards: one for excellence in building construction called the New York State Exam Award, and the other for general excellence and progress.

When Natalie graduated, her father cut out an article from the *New York Times* that gave statistics on women in architecture and showed it to Natalie. He wanted to make it clear to her that architecture was a profession in which there were very few women, it would be difficult for her to find work, and it would be a challenge to work in a profession where she was a minority. But that did not deter Natalie; she was hired right out of Columbia. Architect Morris Ketchum, who was also a Columbia graduate, went to the school and asked at the office for somebody to work for him, and the school sent Natalie. Ketchum's was one of the first firms in New York City doing modern architecture, and Natalie was thrilled.

However, Natalie's work environment was not always pleasant, and a male coworker named Joe Boaz made unwelcome sexual advances toward her that she rebuffed. After nine months, Natalie suffered her first life setback. She explained what happened that day:

> After working my butt off for nine months, I got fired. Mr. Ketchum asked me to come over to his office and he told me I would have to leave. That just came right

out of the blue and I couldn't understand it. He said that
Joe Boaz was very disturbed with having me work in the
office. I didn't respond to his advances, so he had gone to
Mr. Ketchum and told him to ask me to leave."

At 23 years old, Natalie overcame this blatantly unfair and
sexist treatment and began working for Skidmore, Owings &
Merrill (SOM), where she remained for the following 20 years.
Still, things weren't always easy there. As one of the few women
in the design office, she took the discrimination she faced personally, on occasion even escaping to the restroom to cry in
private.

One of her first major projects was the design of the Terrace Plaza Hotel, the first modernist building in Cincinnati. A
new concept at the time, the building had mixed uses. Bond and
JC Penney were on the first seven floors. The hotel occupied
the remaining floors, along with a restaurant and outdoor plaza
with skating rink. The top floor was the round Gourmet Room.
About the Terrace Plaza, Natalie said, "The first publicity for
the hotel design was in the December 1946 *Architectural Forum*.
That issue includes sketches, done by me, and of course, all the
consultants were listed and Mr. Skidmore and Bill Brown. The
Terrace Plaza was widely published, that's true, but I don't think
my name was ever mentioned."

Natalie married in 1945 and had her first of four children in
1948. In September 1951, she was awarded a Fulbright Scholarship and moved to France with her husband and three-year-old
son. On the Fulbright, she did studio work at Beaux-Arts. While
overseas, she was asked to design several US consulate buildings in Germany, which led to Natalie and her family moving to
Germany. In March 1953, they moved back to the United States,
where Natalie returned to the SOM office, and in June she had

another son. In describing the expectation at work at that time in a 2004 SOM article, Natalie said, "I had four children between 1948 and 1957, which was when all these buildings were done. I went to the hospital from the office and then I came back to the office a week after that. No maternity leave."

At SOM, Natalie was the project designer on many buildings for the architect Gordon Bunshaft: Lever House and corporate offices for Pepsi-Cola, Connecticut General Life Insurance, and Union Carbide. In a 2010 interview with Steffan Schmidt, when Natalie was asked about the climate in this male-dominated field, she had a very matter-of-fact yet sometimes contradictory

JEANNE GANG

In 2010, Jeanne Gang designed and built the 82-story Aqua Tower in Chicago, breaking Natalie de Blois's record for the tallest building in Chicago designed by a woman, which had been Equitable Life Assurance. Aqua Tower also breaks the record for the tallest building in the world designed by a woman-owned company. As a child growing up in Belvidere, Illinois, Jeanne would take road trips with her father, a civil engineer, to bridges and architectural landmarks. After graduating from the University of Illinois and Harvard Graduate School of Design, she finally settled in Chicago and started her own firm, Studio Gang Architects, in 1997. About her design theory, Jeanne says, "I see architecture as part of a bigger system. Every building is not just an object—it's connected to an environment about it. The way I work is kind of like a detective, to find all of the factors that could form the building. My philosophy of design is really about making some kind of poetry out of all those factual and scientific criteria."

view of things, saying, "It wasn't tough. I accept it. There's no doubt about it. I was discriminated [against] and I was told I couldn't go to meetings. I couldn't go to lunch with them. I was told I couldn't go to the clubs with them. That was just it."

About her work for Gordon Bunshaft, Natalie said, "He didn't seem to discriminate. He in no way treated me differently than he did anybody else. When he introduced me to the clients he would say, 'This is my best designer and . . . she's going to work on the project.' So that was fine. He wrote a book, Gordon Bunshaft. He didn't say a damn thing about me. I mean I didn't exist."

After working on the Union Carbide building in Manhattan, Natalie was asked to appear on the television program *To Tell the Truth*. A "jury" was told that one of three contestants had just designed a 52-story building, the Union Carbide building. They had to try to figure out which person was actually the designer. Natalie was finally getting some fame for her accomplishments.

Natalie and her husband divorced in 1960. Four years later, now with four sons, she moved to Chicago and became an associate partner at the Chicago SOM office. Ten years later, after 30 years of working in others' shadows, Natalie left SOM. She became an active member of the American Institute of Architects' Task Force on Women. Her presentation "Role Conflict: Professional, Mother, and Wife" received a lot of attention. In her oral history, Natalie explained that her presentation was so popular because everybody always wanted to know how she did it. She said, "How do I bring up four children and work full time as well? Well, I had no alternative. I had divorced my husband in 1960. . . . I had to work. My husband didn't support me or the children. I liked my work and I liked my children. It wasn't a matter of how I would do that."

Juggling her kids and work was not always easy, though. One Saturday when she was still working at SOM, she had to pack

Mario Salvadori, Natalie de Blois, and Philip Johnson in 1948.
Courtesy of Natalie De Blois and SOM

her children in the backseat of her car and drive to Connecticut to discuss with Gordon Bunshaft an architectural model for the Connecticut General building. Because his dog was running around in the yard, Bunshaft had Natalie leave the children out in the car while they discussed work. When it was time for the building's opening, Natalie, pregnant with her third son, was told not to attend the opening if she hadn't had the baby yet because she was an embarrassment to them. At the time, it was not socially acceptable to be working, especially working on a large office-building design, while pregnant.

After leaving SOM in Chicago, Natalie joined the Houston, Texas, firm of Neuhaus & Taylor. From 1980 to 1993, she also taught at the University of Texas at Austin. Natalie was the founding member of Chicago Women in Architecture and started groups in Houston and Austin.

Natalie de Blois retired in 1994 after a 50-year career in architecture. Though she had worked at SOM for 30 years, she did not receive a pension (payments made after retirement) like her male associates simply because she was a woman.

Natalie felt that her biggest contributions were that she was an architect who actually worked on large-scale building projects, as opposed to private residences, and that she had been a mentor for other women. In 2005, Natalie returned to Chicago and moved into the Mies van der Rohe-designed Promontory Apartments one block away from Lake Michigan. She frequently attended cultural events and functions put on by the Chicago Women in Architecture, the group she helped found in the mid-1970s. Natalie often ran into former students and occasionally met strangers who told her about a young woman they knew who she inspired. Natalie died on July 22, 2013 in Chicago, at age 92.

LEARN MORE

Oral history of Natalie de Blois by Natalie de Blois and Betty J. Blum (Art Institute of Chicago, 2004)

ZAHA HADID

Contemporary Architecture Star

Zaha Mohammed Hadid was one of the most celebrated architects of the 21st century, whose contemporary art museum in Cincinnati, Ohio, was called "the most important American building to be completed since the Cold War" by the *New York Times*. But Zaha nearly quit architecture in defeat just before her career took off.

Zaha Mohammed Hadid, born on October 31, 1950, in Baghdad, Iraq, was raised in an intellectual family, where education and the understanding of other cultures were paramount. Her parents were both from Mosul, Iraq. Zaha's father, Mohammed Hadid, was a leading liberal Iraqi politician. Her mother, Wajiha, was from a wealthy Mosul family and taught Zaha how to draw.

Zaha Hadid.
©2011 by Simone Cecchetti

Zaha attended Catholic school. Though taught by nuns, the students and their religions were quite diverse. Zaha said in an interview with *Newsweek*, "the Muslim and Jewish girls could go out and play when the other girls went to chapel." When she was 16, she was sent to Switzerland for a year and then to London to study.

Growing up in a region known as the cradle of civilization had an enormous impact on Zaha. Her world was filled with living history, and picnic trips to the ancient city of Samarra in southern Iraq, where the Tigris and Euphrates Rivers meet. When Zaha was 11, she became fascinated by photos she saw of the Marsh Arabs, inhabitants of the marshes of southern Iraq who live in arched homes constructed of reeds. The photos came from the books of Wilfred Thesiger, an English explorer and friend of her father. When her father took her to visit the places in the book, she knew that she wanted to become an architect. She recalled in the *Guardian*, "My father took us to see the Sumerian cities. Then we went by boat, and then on a smaller one made of reeds to visit villages in the marshes. The beauty of the landscape—where sand, water, reeds, birds, buildings, and people all somehow flowed together—has never left me." The area was in the region of Sumer, where architecture first began in 3000 BC.

There were other influences on Zaha's design aesthetic as well. Zaha described to the *Sunday Times Magazine* how an architect friend of the family—the son of her father's best friend—was asked to design Zaha's aunt's house. The young man created an architectural model that was stationed in Zaha's home, and it fascinated her. She recalled, "I was very young, and I was very intrigued by this thing. I might have thought it was a doll's house. But also—my mother had great taste, we got this new furniture—Italian, late '50s, fantastic furniture. I was very intrigued by all this. I was beginning to see things that were different."

In 1968, Zaha went to college at the American University in Beirut, Lebanon, and got a bachelor's degree in mathematics. Her family left Iraq after the rise of the dictator Saddam Hussein and Iraq's war with Iran. Zaha moved to London and became a student at the Architectural Association School of Architecture. The school had a very loose structure, where students were left on their own to design projects. They learned by being mentored by their teachers, generally world-renowned architects. Zaha sought help from Oscar Niemeyer, a legendary architect from South America and a Pritzker Prize winner. Zaha admired his fearless designs, which pushed the limits of shape and incorporated flowing forms of concrete.

After graduation, Zaha joined her teacher Rem Koolhaas at his firm called "Office of Modern Architecture." She opened her own architectural practice in 1980 and taught at the AA School of Architecture. Most of her designs were conceptual, but her first building was built in 1994, the Vitra Fire Station in Germany

KAZUYO SEJIMA: ANOTHER INTERNATIONAL ARCHITECTURE STAR

Born in 1956 in Ibaraki prefecture, Japan, Kazuyo Sejima received her architectural degree from Japan Women's University. Her Tokyo-based design firm, Sejima and Nishizawa and Associates, has worked on several projects in Germany, France, England, the Netherlands, the United States, and Spain. In 2010 she was awarded the Pritzker Prize with her partner, Ryue Nishizawa.

(the fire department later moved out and a chair museum moved in). The design, with its sharply angled planes, looks like a bird in flight. The building was critically well received.

Despite a successful start, Zaha thought about quitting architecture in 1995. After her design for an ultramodern opera house on Cardiff Bay in the United Kingdom won a competition, the design was rejected by the Millennium Commission who said it was flawed by "uncertainties." The truth is that Cardiff politicians, still stuck in the 1970s with their conservative political and architectural ideals, protested the design. Zaha's proposal was too revolutionary for the city fathers, though design critics applauded it. She told the *London Evening Standard*, "It was such a depressing time. I didn't look very depressed maybe but it was very dire. I made a conscious decision not to stop, but it could have gone the other way." She thought about becoming a painter or a teacher.

Her design practice took a gigantic leap when Zaha won the competition to design the Rosenthal Center for Contemporary Art in Cincinnati. Her first commission in the United States was also the first American museum designed by a woman. Completed in 2003, it was this work that the *New York Times* called "the most important American building to be completed since the Cold War." Other high-profile projects that Zaha designed include the Car Park Terminus in France, the Bergisel Ski Jump in Austria, the BMW Central Building in Germany, the Hotel Puerta America interiors in Spain, the Ordrupgaard Museum extension in Copenhagen, and the Phaeno Science Centre in Germany.

Zaha's architectural designs tend to have fluid shapes, and the buildings appear to flow effortlessly into their building sites. She felt that her designs are best shown through paintings rather than architectural drawings. Appearing to morph and change shape as one moves through the space, her buildings take on a science fiction–like feel. The advent of computer-aided design allowed architects and engineers to realize the out-of-this-world buildings. Engineering the architectural designs required substantial time and money, but slowly clients were ready to invest in Zaha's work.

On May 31, 2004, Zaha was awarded architecture's most prestigious award, the Pritzker, for her body of work and contributions to architecture, at the State Hermitage Museum of St. Petersburg, Russia. She was the first woman and, at 54, the youngest architect to receive this award. Then in 2010 and 2011, Zaha was awarded the Royal Institute of British Architects Stirling Prize for excellence in architecture. For the 2012 Olympics, Zaha designed the dramatically curved London Aquatics Centre, the first thing people saw as they entered Olympic Park.

When asked about the job of an architect, Zaha told the *Guardian*, "If it doesn't kill you, then you're no good. I mean, really—you have to go at it full time. You can't afford to dip in and out." Zaha spoke bluntly about the challenges of being a woman architect, saying, "When women break off to have babies, it's hard for them to reconnect on the big scale. And when [women] do succeed, the press, even the industry press, spend far too much time talking about how we dress, what shoes we're wearing, who we're meant to be seeing [dating]."

Despite these obstacles, Zaha Hadid rose to the top of her field, also finding time to teach at many institutions: Harvard University's Graduate School of Design, the University of Illinois at Chicago School of Architecture, Ohio State University's Knowlton School of Architecture, Columbia University in New York City, Yale School of Architecture, the University of Applied Arts in Vienna, and many other universities around the world. In 2012, she was appointed Dame Commander of the Order of the British Empire for services to architecture (so technically her name is Dame Zaha Hadid).

Zaha was firmly committed to her unique style. She told the *Guardian*, "I can be my own worst enemy. As a woman, I'm expected to want everything to be nice, and to be nice myself. A very English thing. I don't design nice buildings—I don't like them. I like the architecture to have some raw, vital, earthy quality."

> "I don't design nice buildings—I don't like them. I like architecture to have some raw, vital, earthy quality."

In addition to her architectural projects, Zaha worked on several high-profile interior and product designs: a sofa for an Italian furniture company, shoes for Melissa and Lacoste, jewelry for Swarovski, and many others. She even designed a

Pierres Vives in Montpellier, France.
©2012 by Iwan Baan

high-end fashion designer's runway for Paris Fashion Week. Yet, she maintains a down-to-earth, practical sensibility as well.

This earthy yet practical sensibility was also exhibited in the design of the first public building in France designed by Zaha, the Pierres Vives building, inaugurated in Montpellier on September 12, 2012. The streamlined concrete-and-glass structure houses three civic institutions in a single location: the public archives, a multimedia library, and the sports department. The design is inspired by the idea of a "tree of knowledge" as an organizational diagram. The archives are the base of the trunk, reaching out through the library, with the sports department on top where the trunk becomes much lighter. The branches are the entrances into the different areas.

About her future as an architect, Zaha said, "I started out trying to create buildings that would sparkle like isolated jewels; now I want them to connect, to form a new kind of landscape, to flow together with contemporary cities and the lives of their peoples." Zaha died on March 31, 2016, at age 65.

LEARN MORE

Zaha Hadid: Complete Works by Zaha Hadid and Aaron
   Betsky (Rizzoli, 2009)
Zaha Hadid: Form in Motion (Philadelphia Museum of Art) by
   Kathryn B. Hiesinger (Yale University Press, 2011)
The official website of Zaha Hadid Architects, www
   .zaha-hadid.com

MARILYN JORDAN TAYLOR

Building the Future

Growing up in a small Iowa town of 1,432 people, Marilyn Jordan didn't see a big city until she was 10 and her family moved to Washington, DC. In a 2008 article for the *Pennsylvania Gazette*, she recalled, "When I saw a city, I was just mesmerized. I think that the sense of opportunity that cities still offer makes them profoundly compelling places." In DC, her father took her to see the new Dulles International Airport, and Marilyn felt a powerful connection to the building.

Marilyn was born in Montezuma, Iowa, on March 31, 1949. Her parents always thought that Marilyn would become a lawyer, her family's profession. She studied government at Radcliffe College and graduated in 1969. But when Marilyn's parents

Marilyn Jordan Taylor.
Courtesy of Marilyn Jordan Taylor

noticed her interest in and passion for architecture, they allowed her to change course. She received her master's in architecture in 1974 from the University of California, Berkeley, and quickly joined Skidmore, Owings & Merrill (SOM), in the firm's Washington, DC, office. Eleven years later, she was made a partner and moved to New York City to head an expanded urban design and planning practice within SOM. She received a prestigious David Rockefeller Fellowship from the Partnership for New York City in 1995.

Marilyn Taylor has led Skidmore, Owings & Merrill's Urban Design and Planning practice in such projects as Columbia

DEBORAH BERKE

Deborah Berke was the first recipient of the University of California, Berkeley (Marilyn's alma mater), College of Environmental Design (CED) inaugural 2012 Berkeley-Rupp Architecture Professorship and Prize, a $100,000 honor reserved for someone who has made a significant contribution to promoting the advancement of women in the field of architecture and who promotes community building and sustainability. Deborah has been a professor at Yale since 1987, and her design work includes retail stores, offices, private residences, and remodels of older buildings. In praising Deborah, Marilyn Taylor said, "Deborah Berke is an extraordinary architect, whose works are singularly evocative and successful. Throughout her career she has been teacher and practitioner, using each talent to strengthen the other. CED will enjoy her remarkable presence as both role model and provocative. She'll be great as the first architect selected in this wonderful new appointment."

University's Manhattanville Master Plan, the East River Water-front Master Plan, the reclamation of Con Ed's East River sites for mixed-use development, the new research building at Memorial Sloan-Kettering, and the new urban campus for John Jay College. She also founded and led Skidmore, Owings & Merrill's airports and transportation practice, which has become an industry leader in designing and implementing worldwide transportation facilities. Some of her airport projects in the United States include: Terminal 4 at JFK, Continental Airlines at Newark, and the expansion of Washington, DC's Dulles International Airport—the same airport that had so inspired her as a girl. Her international airport projects include SkyCity at Hong Kong International Airport and the Ben Gurion Airport in Tel Aviv, as well as the new Terminal 3 at Singapore's Changi Airport.

Through her work, Marilyn has shaped the landscape of New York. Excited by cities, in a 2009 article for *Penn Current*, a University of Pennsylvania newspaper, she said:

> I loved working on Wall Street with the incredible energy of the markets, the history of Trinity Church and the harbor 270 degrees around. I love living on Washington Square Park. The park is so strong, especially when the trees are out, that the cacophony of buildings all around blends it into a great urban place. I like the small-scale streets of the Society Hill neighborhood, the extraordinary housing stock of Philadelphia—which you find in Capitol Hill in Washington, as well. I love standing at the base of the US Capitol, which I did for the first time when John Kennedy was being sworn in, and being inspired.

Her passion for building around the world is far-reaching. She has said:

I'm incredibly proud of the new Changi Airport that SOM did for Singapore, which is one of the most extraordinary examples of the commitment of a government to investment in infrastructure. I love the markets—I was just in the souk [shopping area] in Marrakesh, Morocco. I love the entrepreneurial spirit. I love any place where the tourists are outnumbered by the locals, but still it's so unique and authentic that tourists come without overrunning it. I love the genuine places that people make."

In 2001, Marilyn became SOM's first female chairman. She was appointed chair of the Urban Land Institute in 2005, the first woman and the first architect to head the prestigious research organization. In 2007, *Crain's New York Business* named her one of the "Most Powerful Women in New York."

Marilyn's late husband, Brainerd Taylor, was an urban planner. Their two children are following in their footsteps; her son is going to architecture school, and her daughter has an urban studies degree. When Marilyn wants to get out of the city for a rest, she heads to her log cabin in New Hampshire. She feels that she is a very lucky person because she's never had to sit at a desk. She's always been able to travel, and works with intelligent and principled people.

> "I'm not really interested in being a 'starchitect.' My hope is to be an effective advocate for making the city a better place for everyone."

Marilyn told *Crain's*, "I'm not really interested in being a 'starchitect.' My hope is to be an effective advocate for making the city a better place for everyone." Marilyn explained, "Cities

Marilyn and recent graduates from High Speed Rail Studio, meeting with Vice President Joe Biden in 2012 to talk about their proposal for a national high-speed rail network for the Northeast Corridor.
Courtesy of Marilyn Jordan Taylor

offer so much—a sense of mobility, economic, social, and physical. That makes them so compelling."

In May 2008, Marilyn became the dean of the University of Pennsylvania School of Design, though she was still a consulting partner with SOM, where she focused on mentoring. Marilyn helped lead the next generation of architects and designers. She focused not just on the buildings but on their impact on the environment, society, and the economy. She took a big-picture view, considering issues such as energy and climate change as they related to her work.

In 2013, Penn's School of Design created new courses to allow students to help redesign infrastructure and discover new ways to build and restructure cities in response to the ever-changing

Dean Marilyn Jordan Taylor with recent master's of city and regional plan-
ning graduates Boris Lipkin (left) and Matthew Rao from her High Speed
Rail studio, co-taught with architect Robert Yaro.
Courtesy of Jamie Diamond, MFA '08/PennDesign

environment, such as working to create more sustainable cities in response to Hurricane Sandy. Marilyn helped implement
the program and taught one of the courses, which focused on
restructuring of the tunnels under Penn Station, which were
shut down for several days in the wake of Hurricane Sandy,
as the tunnels were flooded. Though Marilyn's term as dean
at Penn's School of Design ended in June 2016, with her vast
experiences in the contemporary professional design world and
focus on cities, she continues to help educate the architects of
our future.

LEARN MORE

*Architecture Is Elementary: Visual Thinking Through Architec-
tural Concepts* by Nathan B. Winters (Gibbs Smith, 2005)
The Architect: Women in Contemporary Architecture by Maggie Toy with a preface by Peter Pran (Watson-Guptill,
2001)

PART TWO

ENGINEERS

BEFORE ENGINEERING WAS recognized as a formal profession, women with engineering skills turned to inventing. One of the earliest women inventors was Hypatia of Alexandria. In the early 15th century, Hypatia invented several scientific instruments, including the hydrometer, an instrument used to measure the specific gravity of liquids. Englishwoman Sarah Guppy patented a design for safer suspension bridge foundations in 1811 and had 10 other patents. In 1813, Tabitha Babbitt, a Shaker woman from Massachusetts, invented the first circular saw after watching her brothers wasting energy with a two-man saw. She invented other items, but her strong religious faith did not allow for her to apply for patents.

The word "engineering" was first used in the 15th century as a military term to describe the creation of devices for war, such as launching projectiles. During the Renaissance, engineering took on a more civilian role and involved the construction of Italian canals, and roads and bridges in France, hence the creation of the civil engineer. Engineering began to be taught in the late 18th and early 19th centuries. In 1747, The École National des Ponts et Chaussées (National School of Bridges and Roads) in France was created to teach military and civil engineering, which was modeled after the curriculum at the US West Point Military Academy created in 1802. Rensselaer Polytechnic Institute (RPI) introduced civil engineering in 1824.

In 1876, Elizabeth Bragg graduated from the University of California with a degree in civil engineering and became the first woman engineering graduate. In 1893, Bertha Lamme became the second woman engineering graduate with her degree in mechanical engineering from Ohio State University. As with architecture, engineers started societies to professionalize their practice. In 1880, the American Society of Mechanical Engineers (ASME) was founded. Nora Stanton Blatch Barney was the first woman to become a junior member of the American Society of Civil Engineers in 1906, but it wasn't until 1927 that Elsie Eaves became the first woman to achieve full membership rank. A rise in the number of women in engineering didn't occur until World War II, when men went off to war and industries needed professionals at home to engineer planes, ships, and supplies for the war effort. Like "Rosie the Riveter" in the machine shops, women engineers were needed on the drafting tables.

Today, engineers apply scientific, mathematical, economic, social, and practical knowledge to design and build structures, machines, devices, systems, materials, and processes. There are 25 different engineering and engineering technology majors offered in American universities. Engineering used to be dominated by men, and though the statistics are getting better, there is still a long way to go. The National Science Foundation's *Women, Minorities, and Persons with Disabilities in Science and Engineering* report reveals that in 2008, 41 percent of incoming male college students planned to major in science and engineering, compared to 30 percent of incoming female students. In 2010, the numbers remained similar: 44 percent of men and

33 percent of women planned to major in the sciences. In biology and social and behavioral sciences, there are more women enrolled than men; whereas in engineering, physics, and computer science, men greatly outnumber the women. In addition, the Congressional Commission on the Advancement of Women and Minorities in Science, Engineering, and Technology Development reported in September 2000 that women are about twice as likely as their male colleagues to leave the engineering workforce after a few years (25 percent compared with 12 percent). Of the 60 to 80 students who take professor Angela Bielefeldt's civil engineering class at the University of Colorado at Boulder, she says, only 10 to 12 are generally women.

While master's degrees in engineering awarded to women hovered at 22.6 percent in 2010, a slight dip from 2008 and 2009 levels, bachelor's degrees in the engineering field among women climbed to 18.1 percent, and more engineering doctorates—22.9 percent—were awarded to women than at any time in the past, according to the American Society for Engineering Education.

With a rapidly growing population and aging infrastructure, our nation needs all our creative and technical minds, male and female. As the pioneers in these pages prove, women can build too.

ENGINEERING AND ENGINEERING
TECHNOLOGY COLLEGE MAJORS

The National Academy of Engineering has organized 12 engineering categories. Members are required to select primary and, if needed, secondary affiliations. The scope of each discipline incorporates a diverse area of work. Four main disciplines account for two-thirds of the degrees handed out each year: civil, computer, electrical, and mechanical engineering. The next four disciplines account for one-fifth of all degrees handed out each year: aerospace, biomedical, chemical, and industrial/manufacturing engineering. Fewer than 10 percent of engineering degrees handed out each year include those in agricultural, architectural, engineering management, engineering physics/engineering science, environmental, general engineering studies, materials, mining, nuclear, and petroleum engineering.

Civil Engineering (CE)—applied to public works/infrastructure and buildings/structures.

Areas of specialization: construction management, environmental engineering, geotechnical engineering, structural engineering, surveying, transportation engineering, and water resources engineering

Computer Engineering (CompE)—applied to computers, computation, communication, and information science.

Areas of specialization: artificial intelligence, computer architecture, computer design and engineering, computer theory, information systems, operating systems and networks, robotics, software applications, and software engineering

Electrical Engineering (EE)—applied to all things electrical/electronic: electronic devices, electrical systems, electrical energy, and more.

Areas of specialization: communications, computer engineering, digital systems, electric power, electronics, robotics, and control systems

Mechanical Engineering (ME)—applied to machines, structures, devices, mechanical systems, and energy conversion systems.

Areas of specialization: solid mechanics, fluid mechanics, thermodynamics, and mechanical design

Aerospace Engineering (AeroE)—applied to aeronautical, astronautical, and space systems.

Areas of specialization: aerodynamics, structural design and materials selection, propulsion systems, and guidance-and-control systems

Bioengineering (BioE) and Biomedical Engineering (BiomedE)— applied to biological and medical systems.

Areas of specialization: biomaterials, biomechanics, biotechnology, clinical engineering, and medical devices/equipment

Chemical Engineering (ChemE)—applied to chemical systems, from molecules and microsystems to industrial plants to ecosystems.

Areas of specialization: biotechnology, environmental engineering, petroleum and natural gas, polymers, and process control systems

(continued on next page)

(continued from previous page)

Industrial Engineering (IE) and Manufacturing Engineering (ManE)—applied to efficiency or how to design, organize, implement, and operate the basic factors of production.

Areas of specialization: ergonomics / human factors, facility design, management decision-making / operations research, manufacturing engineering, quality control, work design, and worker productivity

AMERICA'S TOP 10 ENGINEERING SCHOOLS

Based on a 2013 *U.S. News and World Report* survey sent to nearly 200 engineering schools that grant doctoral degrees in engineering, school deans and deans of graduate studies rated their top 10 engineering schools in the United States. The ranking process is rather subjective; different colleges are known for various specialties, such as civil engineering, green engineering, research, and so on. Currently, there are just over 1,000 engineering schools in the United States.

Top 10 Undergraduate Engineering Programs
1. Massachusetts Institute of Technology
2. Stanford University
3. California Institute of Technology
4. University of California, Berkeley
5. Georgia Institute of Technology
6. University of Illinois at Urbana-Champaign
7. University of Michigan
8. Carnegie Mellon University
9. Cornell University
10. Princeton University

Top 10 Graduate Engineering Programs
1. California Institute of Technology
2. Carnegie Mellon University
3. Georgia Institute of Technology
4. Massachusetts Institute of Technology
5. Purdue University
6. Stanford University
7. University of California, Berkeley
8. University of Illinois at Urbana-Champaign
9. University of Michigan
10. University of Southern California
    (Viterbi School of Engineering)

EMILY WARREN ROEBLING

She Built *the* Bridge

While growing up in the New York town of Cold Springs, Emily Warren could hear the side-wheelers blowing their whistles from the nearby Hudson River. Emily had no idea that some 25 years later, the great steamboat the *Mary Powell* would travel down the river, empty into the Upper Bay of the New York City Harbor, and sail under the Brooklyn Bridge she designed.

Born on September 23, 1843, Emily was the second-youngest of 12 children. After her father died, when Emily was 15, her older brother Gouverneur vowed to his mother that he would spend his money to advance his brothers and sisters. Gouverneur Warren, who later became a general in the US Army, paid

Emily Warren Roebling.
Special Collections and University Archives, Rutgers University Libraries
The Frank Lloyd Wright Preservation Trust

for Emily's tuition at the all-girls preparatory school George-town Visitation Convent in Washington, DC.

Emily's studies in prep school were wide-ranging and included ancient and modern history, geography, mythology, composition, French, algebra, geometry, bookkeeping, astronomy, botany, meteorology, chemistry, and geology. She also had classes in housekeeping, domestic economy, crochet, tapestry, embroidery, watercolor, piano, and guitar—because these classes, it was assumed, would make her "marriage material." She graduated in 1860 with the highest honors.

At the age of 20, while visiting Gouverneur, Emily attended a military ball. There, she met civil engineer Washington Roebling, an aide serving under her brother in the Civil War. It was love at first sight, and in less than a year they were married. For two years, the newlyweds lived in Cincinnati while Washington oversaw the construction of his engineer father John Roebling's Ohio River Bridge. They also lived in Europe for two years so Washington could study bridge-construction techniques to aid his father on his new project, the Brooklyn Bridge. While in Germany, Emily gave birth to their son and only child, John A. Roebling II.

In the 1880s, a bridge that could span the East River from Brooklyn to the vastly growing Manhattan Island was becoming a necessity. The congestion of hundreds of boats crossing the river to take passengers from Brooklyn to their jobs in Manhattan had become dangerous, and was impossible during freezing or foggy conditions. After years of debate, the final approval for John Roebling's design of the Brooklyn Bridge came in June 1869.

Just a few days later, John Roebling's foot was accidentally crushed between a ferryboat and a piling while he was surveying one of the bridge tower sites. When he died two weeks later, his son Washington Roebling was appointed chief engineer and took over the entire bridge project. Wanting to help her husband and aided by her strong math skills, Emily began to study civil engineering topics such as strength of materials, cable construction, stress analysis, and physics. During construction, Washington contracted compression sickness, a new illness that was incapacitating bridge workers. Paralyzed and suffering from several other conditions, he was bedridden for the remaining years of the Brooklyn Bridge construction. For 11 years, Emily Roebling handled all areas of Washington's position as chief, while also taking care of her husband and their young son.

At first, Emily's role consisted of keeping records, answering mail, delivering messages, and checking on the construction. She also had to assure all people involved that her husband was able to complete the project in his condition, hiding the severity of his illness.

Emily grew to understand the mathematics and engineering needed to build the bridge. She knew how to speak about catenary curves, stress analysis, and cable construction—so well that many thought she was the chief engineer. In an article in the *New York Times* in 1883, an anonymous family friend spoke out about Emily's involvement on the project: "As soon as Mr. Roebling [was] stricken with that peculiar fever which has since prostrated him, Mrs. Roebling applied herself to the study of engineering and she succeeded so well that in a short time she was able to assume the duties of chief engineer."

The same 1883 article further describes the reaction of a group of men who appeared at the Roebling house expecting to consult with Mr. Roebling on the construction of new steel and iron structures: "Their surprise was great when Mrs. Roebling sat down with them, and by her knowledge of engineering, helped them out with their patterns and cleared away difficulties that had for weeks been puzzling their brains."

Emily participated in many ceremonial duties in her husband's place. In December 1881, Emily led the first walk on a small walkway under the actual bridge across the East River. The plank was only about five feet wide and winter winds were blowing. Stepping off from the Brooklyn tower, she was followed by Mayor James Howell of Brooklyn and Mayor William Russell Grace of New York City, with assistant engineers and reporters close behind. When they reached the New York City tower, several bottles of champagne were opened, and they all drank to the health of Mrs. Roebling. When Ferdinand de Lesseps, the French diplomat who created the Suez Canal, came to town, he wanted to see the bridge. Later that evening, Emily was one of his escorts to a grand banquet in his honor.

In January 1882, when Seth Low took office as the newly elected mayor of Brooklyn, he tried to have Washington Roebling fired from the Brooklyn Bridge project. Washington hadn't been to the site since 1872, and it seemed that his wife had taken over the job. Emily spoke to the American Society of Civil Engineers and convinced them that her husband should not be replaced. She was the first woman to ever speak to the male-dominated group. A week before the bridge's official opening, Emily was given the honor of being the first person to cross the bridge by vehicle. In a new Victorian horse-drawn carriage driven by a coachman, Emily crossed over the bridge from Brooklyn to New York City. She took a live rooster along with her, as a symbol of victory. The workmen stopped to cheer and lift their hats as she came riding by.

At the opening ceremony on May 24, 1883, Emily and her son, John, walked across the bridge together. They started from the Brooklyn side with Mayor Low and met President Chester

On the promenade, Brooklyn Bridge, New York.
Library of Congress LC-USZ62-97318

A. Arthur and many dignitaries coming from the New York side. Ships filled the East Bay below. Cannons blasted. Church bells rang. Everyone cheered. The country celebrated the greatest engineering feat in the history of the United States. The *Brooklyn Eagle* called it "the Eighth Wonder of the World—eighth in time but not in significance."

Financier and manufacturer Abram Hewitt, a competitor of the Roeblings, gave the bridge's opening speech. After praising the late John Roebling and Washington Roebling for their accomplishment, Hewitt gave Emily her credit: "It is thus an

THE HUTSON TWINS: FIRST CIVIL ENGINEERS

Twins Mary and Sophie Hutson both completed the requirements for the four-year civil engineering degree at Texas A&M University in 1903. Though women at that time were denied admission, the twins were able to enroll in the program because their father was a professor at the university. At graduation, they were awarded certificates of completion, not actual degrees. In 1963, Texas A&M finally opened its doors to women. Ninety-nine years after the twins completed their degrees, their sons accepted the diplomas on behalf of their mothers at a commencement ceremony.

everlasting monument to the self-sacrificing devotion of woman, and of her capacity for that higher education from which she has been too long disbarred. The name of Mrs. Emily Warren Roebling will thus be inseparably associated with all that is admirable in human nature, and with all that is wonderful in the constructive world of art."

"The name of Mrs. Emily Warren Roebling will thus be inseparably associated with all that is admirable in human nature, and with all that is wonderful in the constructive world of art."

After the bridge was completed, the Roeblings moved to Trenton, New Jersey, and Emily managed the construction of their mansion. Trenton newspapers wrote that a conversation piece in the Roebling home was the infamous rooster, stuffed and mounted, which

Brooklyn Bridge, 1900.
Library of Congress LC-D4-12702

had ridden with Emily on that inaugural trip across the bridge. Emily had an active social life, taking on important roles in the Daughters of the American Revolution, the Huguenot Society, and other civic organizations. She traveled extensively, attending the coronation of Nicholas II in Russia, and was presented to Queen Victoria in London in 1896.

In 1899, at the age of 56, Emily graduated from the Women's Law Class of the New York University. The commencement exercises were held at the concert hall in Madison Square Garden. Emily graduated with high honors and was chosen to read her paper, "A Wife's Disabilities." For the graduation class essay contest, Emily's essay about equal rights for women won her first-prize honors and $50. Later, while Emily's professor, Isaac Franklin Russell, was praising her work, her husband Washington reportedly said, "I never heard her essay until tonight and I do not agree with one word she has said." Surprisingly, after all the work Emily accomplished on the Brooklyn Bridge for her husband, Washington still held the belief that women should not have legal rights.

Emily continued to be a speaker in high demand for several years. In December 1902 she became suddenly ill and died two months later, on February 28, 1903, at age 58. Washington Roebling remarried and lived another 23 years—surprising given all those years of illness while Emily took care of him and the bridge.

May 24, 1953, marked the 70th anniversary of the opening of the Brooklyn Bridge. The city of New York honored Emily, 50 years after her death, for her accomplishment and strength. A ceremonial plaque was dedicated to the memory of Emily Warren Roebling, "whose faith and courage helped her stricken husband." On the bottom of the plaque, it read: BACK OF EVERY GREAT WORK WE CAN FIND THE SELF-SACRIFICING DEVOTION OF A WOMAN.

LEARN MORE

The Great Bridge: The Epic Story of the Building of the Brooklyn Bridge by David McCullough (Simon and Schuster, 1972)

The Roebling Legacy by Clifford Zink (Princeton Landmark Publications, 2011)

Silent Builder: Emily Warren Roebling and the Brooklyn Bridge by Marilyn E. Weigold (Associated Faculty Press, 1984)

LILLIAN MOLLER GILBRETH

The Real *Cheaper by the Dozen*

Lillian Gilbreth—known as "Mother of the Year," "the Greatest Woman Engineer in the World," and "the Mother of Industrial Psychology"—was a towering figure in the public eye from the 1920s to the 1960s. But what the public didn't know was that Lillian's fame was thrust upon her: she was an extremely shy person and was doing what needed to be done to support her family of 12 children. The 1948 movie *Cheaper by the Dozen* portrays her exclusively as a doting wife and mother; in reality, Lillian had her doctorate and profoundly changed the way we interact with the spaces we live and work in today.

Lillian (Lillie) Evelyn Moller Gilbreth was born to German parents Annie Delger and William Moller. The Delger family

Lillian Moller Gilbreth.
Courtesy of Purdue University Libraries, Karnes Archives and Special Collections

came from Germany in 1847, eventually settling in San Francisco around the time of the California Gold Rush. The Mollers made their money by bringing their sugar-refining business from Germany to America.

Eldest son William became smitten with Annie, and they married. Annie immediately got pregnant, but lost the baby. Her second pregnancy was successful, and baby Lillie was born on May 28, 1878. Annie's health was still fragile and a constant concern for William. When Annie would take short trips out of the house, William would pace the floors, leaving Lillie to wonder if her mother was coming back. Annie gave birth to eight more children; five girls, then three boys. Each older daughter had a crib in her room for the sibling who was her responsibility.

In her autobiography, *As I Remember*, Lillian describes herself as a shy child and easily frightened. She was uncomfortable going into town to buy clothes, meeting people, and being in social settings. For Christmas and birthdays, Lillie loved to receive books. Her collection was organized by color and size. To escape from her fears, she read; when she was reading, she was never lonely or unhappy.

Until Lillie was nine years old, her mother taught her at home. In the mornings, first came breakfast, then chores, then the day's lessons. Once in public school, the principal placed her in first grade. Much older than the other students, Lillie was singled out due to her good grades and the responsibilities the teacher gave her, which earned her the "teacher's pet" label. Lillie had few friends, so Valentine's Day was the worst, most embarrassing day of the year. Her mother even tried to secretly send valentines to Lillie. One year, Lillie came home in tears because some boys sent her "comic" valentines teasing her as a "blue stocking"—a girl interested only in studying and books. When girls would come over to her house, they wanted to giggle and whisper, but Lillian showed them her book collection. She decided that if she couldn't be pretty she had to be smart, so she poured herself into her studies.

When Lillian started at Oakland High School in 1892, the family moved to a house farther out of town, which meant Lillie had to ride the streetcar rather than walk to school. The change bothered her, because it was very important to her to be punctual. With her knack for time management and organization beginning to show itself, she would carefully calculate exactly how long the streetcar trip was from home to school.

Still shy but starting to fit in a little better, Lillie was elected vice president of her senior class, and her poems were published in the school paper. She concentrated on her classes and got all As her senior year. She had hopes of going to college like her aunt Annie Flo, and uncles Everett and David, but there was tension in the Moller house. Lillie wrote, "Mama was sympathetic to the idea—she always supported any plan to cultivate one's self. Strangely enough, it was Papa—always so quick to give any child what she wanted—who opposed the idea. His reasoning ran like this, 'Your mother, aunts, grandmothers, never went to college, [and] they are cultivated gentlewomen. Your place is here at home. . . . College is only necessary for teachers and other women who have to make a living. No daughter of mine will have to do that. I can support them!'"

Lillie's father finally gave in on the condition that she could try it for a year. But Lillie excelled and her father soon relented. At the end of senior year, she was disappointed that she didn't make the Phi Beta Kappa list, though she tied with another boy. As part of the 1900 graduating class, Lillian was selected to be one of the commencement speakers; the other two were men. Her subject was "Life—A Means or an End." Her adviser, who had been her linguistics teacher, helped prepare her for her speech. Lillie wrote about his advice: "Don't wear a stiff dress, wear one that is soft and has ruffles. Don't scream. . . . Don't try to imitate a man—speak as a woman." Lillie, who now went by the more dignified Lillian, was the first woman commencement speaker at the University of California, Berkeley.

In the spring of 1902, Lillian got her master's degree in English from Berkeley. After her first year of studies toward a doctorate degree in English, Lillian decided to take a trip to Europe with two friends, Eva and Mary, and a teacher/chaperone, Minnie Bunker. At that time, it was fashionable for young women of social standing to travel to Europe before marrying, as part of their cultural education. Lillian and Eva left Oakland in June 1903. They joined Mary and Minnie in New England for some visiting with relatives and sightseeing.

At the home of Minnie's Aunt Martha, Lillian met Martha's only son, Frank Gilbreth. A self-made man, having worked himself up in the construction industry by implementing time-saving techniques, Frank was 10 years older than Lillian. The group went sightseeing in Frank's Buzz-Wagon, an impressive red sports car. On the second day, the car broke down and needed a new tire. While the men were working on the car, several youngsters started to gather around and became a little unruly. The big sister of nine quickly got the children under control. On the way home, Frank was full of compliments for Lillian, having counted 42 children and one dog under her spell. Upon Lillian's return from her European adventure, Frank proposed to her. They set their wedding date for October 1904, leaving 10 months for preparations. During their months apart, Frank sent Lillian manuscripts to edit and brochures to review, already involving her in his business. After their wedding in San Francisco, they took the train to their honeymoon spot, the World's Fair in St. Louis.

Though Frank Gilbreth didn't have any schooling past high school, he was considered the father of time-motion studies (the study of work habits in all sorts of industries to find ways to increase productivity and make jobs easier).

While working as a bricklayer, he had developed a system of building that radically increased the construction time of houses. At 27, Frank started his own engineering consulting company, Gilbreth Inc., which helped businesses implement efficiency strategies that increased productivity and saved time.

On the train the day after their wedding, Frank declared to Lillian, "I want to teach you about concrete and masonry." Lillian had studied English and was planning on being an English teacher, and had taken very little math and science. She had not expected to be studying on her first day of marriage.

When Lillian was pregnant with their first child, she heard for the first time Frank's vision for their family. Frank, always planning ahead, had decided that they would have six boys and six girls. Coming from a family of nine children, Lillian knew how hard living in a big family could be. However, Frank's prediction came true. While spending most of their time living on the East Coast, Lillian gave birth to 12 children within 19 years. Anne was born in September 1905, followed by Mary Elizabeth, Ernestine, Martha, Frank Jr., Bill, Lillian, Fred, Daniel, John, Robert, and finally Jane in 1922. The Gilbreth household became their laboratory for time motion and efficiency.

The Gilbreth family moved to Rhode Island in 1910; at this time there were four children. The next year, Frank convinced Lillian to get her doctorate in psychology, which would help their time-motion consulting business. While Lillian was preparing her dissertation for her doctoral degree, Anne and Mary came down with diphtheria. Lillian and the other children were quarantined. Anne had a mild case, but five-year-old Mary was weaker and succumbed to the disease. Mary's death hit the family hard.

Lillian submitted her thesis, "The Psychology of Management," to the University of California for publication, but they required that she live on campus during the final year of her doctoral program. Unable to do that, Frank and Lillian finally found a publisher who would accept her thesis manuscript, but only if Lillian used her initials instead of her first name so that no one would know that it was written by a woman. Lillian refused. Brown University was the only large university that would give her a PhD in "applied management."

Lillian had to write another dissertation for the new doctorate degree at Brown. She published her first dissertation on her own in 1914, but the work didn't count toward her doctorate. The book, *Psychology of Management*, covered the psychological aspects of industrial management—the importance of human relations in the workplace and the importance of understanding individual differences among workers. Her book made her a pioneer in the field of what is now known as organizational psychology.

The large Gilbreth family functioned with the same systems that Lillian had learned while growing up in a family of nine children, while also implementing the time management techniques that Lillian and Frank were becoming known for. While working on her doctoral dissertation at Brown, Lillian also ran the business while her husband was away and wrote most of the many books and articles they authored. Frank created an instruction card that spelled out Lillian's weekdays. With the help of her Grandma Martha, they would spend the mornings until 10:00 AM getting the children fed and dressed. Then, Lillian would spend two hours working, two hours with the children and lunch, take a 30-minute nap, spend 30 minutes with an infant, an hour working, an hour with callers, an hour with the children, 30 minutes on miscellaneous tasks, and then an hour for dinner.

Lillian's second dissertation was "Some Aspects of Eliminating Waste in Teaching"; at 400 pages, it was twice the length of her first one. Frank, who was on a steamer crossing the ocean at the time, was unable to attend her graduation ceremony. Arriving home, and before the steamer even reached the dock, he was shouting, "Did you get it?" With the PhD behind Lillian's name, she could now be listed as an author on their papers. They authored more than 50 papers in the following nine years. Previously, publishers wouldn't print her name because she was a woman; they finally allowed her first book, *The Psychology of Management*, to be published under the gender-neutral L. M.

Lillian, holding baby Dan, working at home surrounded by seven children, 1917.
Courtesy of Purdue University Libraries, Karnes Archives and Special Collections

Gilbreth, which was allegedly a compromise. While Lillian and her husband tried to convince publishers to use Lillian's name, another work on the same topic was getting rave reviews. After two years of refusals from publishers, they decided that getting published with a gender-neutral name was better than not getting published at all.

In 1924, Frank was instrumental in launching the first International Congress of Management in Prague. On the way, Lillian and Frank had planned to attend the World Power Conference in London, where Kate Gleason would be the American Society

NORA STANTON BLATCH BARNEY

Not all of the husbands of notable women architects and engineers were supportive of their wives' careers. Nora Stanton, granddaughter of early women's rights leader Elizabeth Cady Stanton, was the first woman admitted to the American Society of Civil Engineers, in 1916. A New York Times article titled WARNS WIVES OF CAREERS, said of Nora's first husband, radio pioneer Lee de Forest, "His matrimonial catastrophe was due to the fact that his wife . . . had persisted in following her career as a hydraulic engineer and an agitator for the cause in which her grandmother, Elizabeth Cady Stanton, was a pioneer, after the birth of her child. He took the position that a woman who had undertaken the obligations of a wife and mother was in duty bound to devote her time to her child or children even at the sacrifice of her career."

Nora remarried and had two more children and enjoyed a successful career as an architect, designing dozens of homes on Long Island in New York.

of Mechanical Engineers' representative. Five days before they were to sail, Frank suffered a fatal heart attack in a phone booth while talking to Lillian. Several of her children were sick with measles and chicken pox, but Lillian handled all the business involved with the funeral in those five days and sailed to Europe to represent the both of them. Elizabeth (Libby) Sanders, a neighbor and Smith College friend of her eldest daughter, went with her as a companion and helper.

After Frank's death, Lillian immediately continued the work that she and her husband had started; she had a large family to support. In her research, she brought time motion and efficiency into the home and kitchen to find the one best way to perform household tasks. Among her many ideas Lillian implemented for aiding the handicapped, she designed an ideal kitchen layout for the disabled homemaker or veteran. Lillian and Frank were sensitive to the needs of the more than 13 million disabled solders who returned from World War I injured. (Frank had once been temporarily paralyzed while recovering from a rheumatism attack.)

In 1926, Lillian was named the first woman member of the American Society of Mechanical Engineers, based on her consulting work, research, publications, lectures, and workshops around the world that defined the area of industrial engineering. When Herbert Hoover ran for president in 1928, Lillian supported him and served as president of the Women's Branch of the Engineers' National Hoover Committee. Hoover and his wife, Lou Henry, were both engineers. Lillian's friend Kate Gleason was honorary vice president, and Mrs. Henry Ford and Mrs. Thomas Edison were officers. Lillian, Kate, and Lou Henry also founded the Engineering Women's Club in 1928, with headquarters in New York City.

Then in 1935, Lillian became a professor of management at Purdue University and the first female professor in the engineering school. As at Gilbreth and Company, she worked with General Electric and other firms to improve the design of kitchens and household appliances. She even created new techniques to help disabled women accomplish common household tasks.

In 1948, two Gilbreth children, Ernestine and Frank, wrote a book about their childhood entitled *Cheaper by the Dozen* that includes humorous stories about the time and motion techniques employed in their large household. The book was an instant success, and Hollywood made a movie of the same title in 1950. The book and movie end at Frank's death, and do not mention Lillian's accomplishments before and after.

Despite that omission, Lillian gained fame as one of the world's great industrial and management engineers, and traveled and worked in many countries of the world. She did not retire from professional work until she was in her 80s. In 1966, she won the Hoover Medal of the American Society of Civil Engineers for distinguished public service by an engineer. She died on January 2, 1972, at the age of 93, the recipient of more than 20 honorary degrees, and she was the first female psychologist ever to have a United States postage stamp issued in her honor.

LEARN MORE

Cheaper by the Dozen by Frank B. Gilbreth Jr. and Ernestine Gilbreth Carey (Thomas Y. Crowell Company, 1948)
Lillian Gilbreth: Redefining Domesticity by Julie Des Jardins (Westview Press, 2012)

KATE GLEASON

Concrete Pioneer

For Kate Gleason, engineering and machinery were second nature. Her father, William Gleason, immigrated to New York City from Ireland in 1848, three years after the great potato famine swept through that country. Eventually settling in Rochester, in upstate New York, he impressed the owner of a machine shop and was hired as an apprentice-in-training. Within a decade he had a new wife and baby boy.

In 1857, with the economy weakened, William and his family moved to Chicago for a better-paying job. But tragedy struck two years later, when William's wife and second child, a one-year-old daughter, both died of tuberculosis. Devastated, William returned to Rochester so that his mother could take care

Kate Gleason.
Courtesy of Jan Gleason

121

of his son, Tom, while William worked at a machine shop and studied mathematics at night school. At 27, he married a young, fellow Irish immigrant named Ellen McDermott. On November 24, 1865, Catherine Anselm Gleason was born. They nicknamed her "Kittie" and then called her Kate when she was older. Over the next few years, William and Ellen had three more children: James, Andrew, and Eleanor.

William started a machine shop of his own with his friend John Connell, and later added partner James Graham, creating Connell, Gleason, and Graham. They manufactured major woodworking machines, such as lathes and planers used to shape and straighten wood. In 1867, William patented his design for a device that held tools in a metalworking lathe and named it Gleason's Patent Tool Rest.

As the company expanded, William disagreed with his partners over the direction the company would take. He felt that they should concentrate more on metalworking tools, due to the high demand from the rapidly growing railroad industry; his partners disagreed. William left and became partner and supervisor at Kidd Iron Works, one of the largest machine shops and foundries in western New York. In 1875, William became the sole owner and renamed it Gleason Works. His son Tom became his right-hand man.

> "I always jumped from a little higher barn, and vaulted a taller fence than did my boy playmates, just to prove that I was as good as they."

Meanwhile, young Kate went to grade school at Nazareth Academy, an all-girls Catholic school. When playing with the neighborhood boys, she resisted the stereotype that girls were second place. "Girls were not considered as valuable as boys; so I always jumped from a little higher barn, and vaulted a taller fence than did my boy playmates, just to prove that I was as good as they," she explained. At nine years old and no doubt influenced by the family business, Kate was reading books on machinery and engineering.

When Kate was 11, her beloved half-brother, Tom, died suddenly of typhoid fever. It was a shock to the family and a blow to Gleason Works. A few days later, Kate heard her parents talking. Her dad, worried about the family business, said, "Oh, if Kate had only been a boy!" Kate's two younger brothers were still too young to work, and her mom thought that Kate should learn about the family business. That Saturday Kate walked down to the machine shop, jumped on a stool, and demanded work. Her dad smiled and gave her some bills to make out. From that day on, Kate helped out in the shop on a regular basis.

Two years later, a banking crisis hit Rochester industries and investments. Due to a drastic slowing of demand, William had to decrease his employees from 150 to three. Kate, then 14 years old, offered to handle the bookkeeping by herself. At the end of that day, Kate's father handed her a dollar bill for her work. Walking home, Kate lost the dollar, but that didn't concern her. The challenge of working for her father's business and the desire to succeed was more important. While attending high school at the Rochester Free Academy, Kate would wake up at 4:00 AM to study before going to school at 8:00 AM. School went until 1:00 PM, when she would eat lunch and then work at the family business until 6:00 PM. Kate helped engineer the new machinery, worked in the shop, and handled all financial matters. Soon, Gleason Works was back on its feet. They had designed special machinery for the oil industry, which was then experiencing a boom.

After high school, and with the business doing well, Kate took and passed the entrance exams to Cornell University's Sibley College of Mechanical Engineering and Mechanic Arts. Being the first woman in the four-year bachelor of engineering program didn't bother Kate. She was used to working at her father's all-male machine shop. Her courses included German, geometry, algebra, trigonometry, drawing, and shop work. All women students at Cornell lived in dorms at Sage College. Henry Sage had given $250,000 to Cornell so that "instruction shall be afforded to young women . . . as broad and as thorough as that now afforded to young men. Women should have the liberty to learn what they can, and to do what they have the power to do." Sage College had strict social and behavioral rules enforced by a woman the female students nicknamed "Warden." Kate complained in a letter to her father that the rules were an insult to the girls.

Back at Gleason Works, its customers were failing and unable to pay their bills, so Kate's father asked her to consider returning to the business for a year, and then continue school later. Kate could not refuse her father but declared that quitting her studies was her "first big sorrow." With her father's letter in hand, Kate sat under a secluded tree on campus and cried and cried. When a concerned classmate asked her what was wrong, she sobbed that she had to leave. He replied, "I'm awfully sorry, but . . . at present I can't be more than a brother to you." After trying to unsuccessfully convince the young man that she was sad about leaving the college, not him, Kate was furious and distraught. Though she had experienced only one year of college, Kate felt it was essential to the profession she wished to pursue. Leaving the other men at the college fueled her determination and drive. She said, "I worked with every bit of energy I possessed."

Kate was soon running the office at Gleason Works and traveling by herself to companies across the Midwest to sell the

Gleason machinery. At 25 she was given the official title of secretary-treasurer to the reorganized Gleason Tool Company, but it was her business and sales sense that grew the company. Kate convinced her father to concentrate on their bevel gear planer, a machine that made gears which could work on a bend. Their machine made gears faster and cheaper than any competitor's. Beveled gears were a very important part of the fast-growing bicycle industry, and a major contributor to the rapidly expanding auto industry.

Though she never did return to Cornell, Kate was always learning and took night classes in mechanical engineering. When traveling around the country selling the Gleason Works gear machinery, she showed companies and manufacturers how the gears worked. Not only did she need to explain the engineering involved with her product, she had to have knowledge of the engineering process at any company on which she called. For her breadth of engineering knowledge, she earned the title "Madame Curie of machine tools."

As Kate turned 29, she was aboard the cattle steamer *Mongolian* on a two-month trip across the Atlantic. Her doctor had recommended a vacation to relax from the stress of her work. He suggested Atlantic City, but Kate reasoned that pursuing business opportunities in Europe would be a better use of her time. She packed one black cashmere dress as her business attire. Kate was the only woman passenger. Fourteen men took turns walking the ship's deck with her, sharing the time equally with the use of a stopwatch. Kate was feeling much better. She traveled to firms in Scotland, England, France, and Germany and returned home successful, with many large orders. Thus, she headed the first movement in America for businesses to expand overseas.

The fact that Rochester played an important role in the women's suffrage movement must have influenced Kate to break out of the traditional Victorian view of a young lady. When she was 22, she had been elected a member of the Fortnightly Ignorance Club, a local professional and businesswomen's club, of which Susan B. Anthony, a friend of Kate's parents, was a member. When Kate was growing up, Anthony gave Kate advice that worked to her advantage. Anthony said, "Any advertising is good. Get praise if possible, blame if you have to. But never stop being talked about." In 1872, Anthony made her hometown a center of the women's suffrage movement when she cast her vote with 14 other women at the Rochester polls. Two weeks later, taking her own advice, she was arrested for breaking a federal law.

In 1903, Anthony gave Kate a gift: the three-volume *History of Woman Suffrage* that Anthony had edited with others. The inscription read, "Kate Gleason, the ideal business woman of whom I dreamed fifty years ago—a worthy daughter of a noble father." Kate's family hosted Anthony's 86th birthday celebration at their home with a brilliant reception. It was to be her last—Anthony died four months later.

After a 35-year career at her family's company, Kate left in 1914. This also marked the time she started to receive many accolades. In 1913, she was elected as a member of the prestigious German Engineering Society, Verein Deutscher Ingenieure, an honor for any American, particularly the first elected woman. That same year she was the first woman elected into the American Society of Mechanical Engineers (ASME). Always following the advice of Anthony, it was reported that she received the award wearing an evening gown and pearls. A few months later, at an ASME dance, she was the only woman member in the midst of 4,000 men. She also was the first woman elected to the Rochester Engineering Society.

Kate was appointed by a bankruptcy court in 1914 to help Ingle Machine Company out of debt. Within two years, the company went from owing $140,000 to being worth over $1 million. When Kate's friend moved overseas to help with the war effort, the First Bank of East Rochester was left without a president. The directors unanimously elected Kate to that position, and she became the first woman head of a national bank without family ties.

Kate had always envisioned constructing low-cost housing in the rapidly growing East Rochester area. She slowly bought up land for her plans. Her first project was to turn seven acres of swampland into a park. She also designed, engineered, and built a country club named Genundawah on the land. In 1919, after World War I ended, a wedding boom of more than one million marriages of returning soldiers led to a housing shortage for these new families. Kate began building a community, which she called "Concrest," that could house the newlyweds.

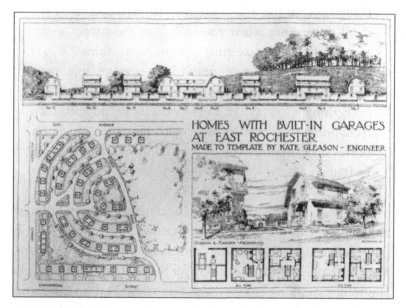

Kate Gleason's "Concrest."
Courtesy of Jan Gleason

> "I had been developing a talent that almost amounted to genius for putting myself in places where other women are not likely to come."

The community was designed to resemble a French village, with homes placed on angles to minimize uniformity on roads wrapped around a hillside. Kate decided to use concrete as the building material for the homes instead of the traditional wood or brick. Earlier, she had witnessed the destruction of Gleason Works' foundry and other nearby factories by fire. The devastation and lost lives affected her deeply. Also, concrete was an economical material.

An advertisement for the houses read:

> Hang up your hat in a home of your own and enjoy the thrill that comes when you look over the happy homestead and proudly exclaim, "It's mine! All mine!" . . . A home with a deed, title, porch light, garage, fine view, fireplace, electricity, green grass, French windows and everything. . . . Play "Home Sweet Home" on your own front porch this summer while you enjoy a ten-mile view of the surrounding country and the cooling breezes are wafted your way.

Kate wanted the entire world to hear of her project. She wrote and spoke at every opportunity. On one occasion, when her ship got stuck in the fog returning from France and Italy, she wired ahead to have a hairdresser ready for her so that she wouldn't be late to her speaking engagement. She arrived on time wearing a Parisian gown and hat to give her, as she said, "moral support in undertaking to tell an audience of men how to build houses."

KATE AND LILLIAN, GOOD FRIENDS

Frank and Lillian Gilbreth occasionally consulted with Gleason Works. On one trip, Kate and Lillian sat in the cab of a small steam engine, and Kate showed Lillian how to run it. Kate applied Frank and Lillian's time and motion techniques to the construction of Concrest houses and saved considerable time and money. Kate and Lillian also sailed together on the *Scythia* from New York on Thursday June 19, 1924, five days after Frank's death. Lillian quickly scheduled a daily four o'clock tea in the Garden Lounge for all the ladies on the ship. Libby Sanders, Lillian's companion, wrote in her diary, "A fascinating person, Miss Gleason, held the stage. She is the jolliest and most adorable person. She knows all there is to know about building houses." Kate, Lillian, and Libby were traveling companions in Europe and also sailed home together, returning to New York in August 1924. Kate and Lillian also traveled together to the World Engineering Congress in Tokyo in 1929. The women were such good friends that Kate even left money to Lillian in her will.

The American Concrete Institute (ACI) must have been impressed with her community at Concrest because they elected her a member. At the time of her death, she was the one and only woman elected to the ACI, proving once again her words, "I had been developing a talent that almost amounted to genius for putting myself in places where other women are not likely to come."

Kate once told a reporter that she had received 200 marriage proposal letters over the years. In a later interview, she explained, "Marriage is a career all by itself. Some women do not find it so. But it would have had to be with me."

She always held strongly to her belief that a businesswoman can work as well as a man, even carving into one of her Moorish chairs the Latin motto POSSUM VOLO ("I can, if I will"). She found that being a woman did not limit her in her career. When she was 60 years old, she said, "When I recall stories told to me by other women struggling for a place in other professions, I insist that engineers are in a class apart."

Kate died on January 9, 1933, at the age of 68. By the standards of that time period, which was about to head into the Great Depression, she died a wealthy woman, with an estate worth over $1.4 million—worth more than $24 million today. In Kate's will, she bequeathed her wealth to more than 70 individuals and organizations.

LEARN MORE

Engineering Legends: Great American Civil Engineers (32 Profiles of Inspiration and Achievement) by Richard Weingardt (American Society of Civil Engineers, 2005)
The Life and Letters of Kate Gleason by Janis F. Gleason (RIT Press, 2010)

MARGARET INGELS

Ruler of the Slide Rule

According to Alice Charlotte Goff's 1946 book *Women Can Be Engineers*, "Margaret Ingels' interest in air conditioning started when she was a tot on her mother's knee. When she observed moisture collecting on a cold glass, her curiosity about the common scientific principle of condensation became insatiable." Margaret's unusual childhood interest in science and her subsequent career in air conditioning would have an enormous impact on the living conditions inside our homes.

Margaret Ingels was born October 25, 1892, in Paris, Kentucky. Her parents were Benjamin Charles and Mary Agnes Wilson Ingels. Her great-great-great-grandmother, Catherine Boone Ingels, had ties to folk hero and frontiersman Daniel

Boone. Maggie, as she was called, attended public school, and in 1911 she enrolled at the University of Kentucky (UK), in Lexington, where she hoped to study architecture. She supposedly had a "flair for construction work." There was no degree program for architecture at UK, so Dean F. Paul Anderson persuaded her to pursue a degree in mechanical engineering as the next best thing. Margaret was known as "one of Dean Anderson's boys." *Scientific American* explained that despite her early interest in air conditioning, "Miss Ingels said that it was no particular astuteness on her part that led her into the engineering field, but only plain, dumb obedience to her family's wishes."

Next to Margaret's photo in *The Kentuckian*, her college yearbook, it read: "'Maggie' has the distinction of being the first and only girl to graduate from the College of Mechanical Engineering. She has not been a hanger-on, but has taken everything in the course from forge to the Senior Trip. While not much given to pushing her views to the front, it has come to light since the war began that she is decidedly pro-'Dutch.'" Maggie's boyfriend for many years was the University of Kentucky's star football player, "Dutch" Charles Christopher Schrader; this may have been an inside joke referencing their relationship.

While Maggie was in college, she served as secretary for several engineering groups and was inducted into the honor society. In 1916, she received a bachelor's degree in mechanical engineering, the first engineering degree received by a woman at the University of Kentucky.

In a *Kentucky Kernel* article titled "Margaret Ingels in Class by Herself," published after she graduated, the reporter asked Margaret if she was sorry that she had studied engineering. Margaret replied, "No, I'm not. There were some things to give up that were hard at the time, but I haven't missed them much. The worst feature is that it keeps me away from the other

Margaret Ingels standing behind a forge (a metal furnace), preparing to work on metal.

University of Kentucky Margaret Ingels Collection (University of Kentucky), circa 1845–1967, 0000UA107-018, Special Collections, University of Kentucky, Lexington

college girls and I haven't made any real girl friends at all." The article continued, "To the all-important question, 'Will you ever marry?' Miss Ingels replied, 'No! It will be four years before another leap year, and by then I hope to be independent.'"

Upon graduation, Margaret's first job was in the traffic-engineering department of the Chicago Telephone Company. She left Chicago and, harkening back to her childhood passion, worked for the Carrier Lyle Heating and Ventilation Corporation in Pittsburgh, Pennsylvania. She left Carrier to return to the University of Kentucky in order to finish a graduate degree in engineering. In 1920 Margaret became the first woman in the nation to receive a graduate degree in mechanical engineering.

After graduation, Margaret was asked to work at the United States Bureau of Mines at the Pittsburgh Laboratory. Her former college dean, Paul Anderson, was the director of the lab and was gathering his former students to work with him. In 1921, he asked Margaret to work with other members of the American Society of Heating and Ventilating Engineers. Her work included field tests for the New York Commission on School Ventilation to evaluate health and attendance in schools, which involved a new portable machine that determined the amount of germ-laden dust.

While working with F. Paul Anderson and O. W. Armspach, Margaret helped develop the Anderson-Armspach dust determinator, which became the industry standard for air filtration. In 1922 she presented a paper titled "Temperature, Humidity and Air Motion Effects in Ventilation" with Anderson at the Annual Meeting of the American Society of Heating and Ventilating Engineers. That same year she also presented "Temperature, Humidity and Air Motion and Standard Method of Testing Dust Removal Efficiencies of Air Washers" with Armspach. Three years following, she presented "Data on Air Dust Determinations." All these studies created standards in the building industry for the cleanliness of the air that we breathe—standards designed to improve

Margaret Ingels and two men sitting at a drafting table, 1916.

University of Kentucky Margaret Ingels Collection (University of Kentucky), circa 1845–1967, 0000UA107-017, Special Collections, University of Kentucky, Lexington

our health, safety, and comfort. Air conditioning played an important part in our nation's history by changing our quality of life and revolutionizing businesses and industries that previously paid little attention to air quality.

Returning to Carrier in 1929, Margaret helped perfect the design for an invention called the sling psychrometer, which is used to read the relative humidity of the air and remains in use today. An article in the *Kentucky Kernel* was complimentary about her initiative in testing a new cigar and cigarette smoke–measuring device. The article read, "Consuming cartons of Camels is quite an ordinary affair for milady of today, but at the time of which we write, [her research] required true courage and an unswerving purpose."

Margaret was invited to Washington, DC, by President Herbert Hoover to attend the President's Conference on Home Building and Home Ownership. At the 1940 meeting of the Women's Continental Congress, she was honored as one of the 100 outstanding women of the nation, along with Eleanor Roosevelt. She received national attention and was invited to the White House, where she was recognized as one of 100 women whose career choice did not exist 100 years ago.

Over the course of her career, Margaret wrote over 45 technical articles for magazines and journals. Between 1950 and 1952, she authored a book about her friend and colleague titled *Willis Haviland Carrier: Father of Air Conditioning*. Margaret gave more than 200 speeches over a 20-year span on engineering and ventilation. Her most well-known talk was entitled "Petticoats and Slide Rules"; she presented it to the Western Society of Engineers in Chicago on September 4, 1952. The presentation included short biographies of the many women engineers who came before her. She said, "The woman who joins the procession of engineers today, tomorrow, and tomorrow's tomorrow benefits by a rich heritage bequeathed to her by those who came before. She assumes automatically the responsibility to further prove that petticoats and slide rules are compatible and she must not carry the responsibility lightly." She went on, "Her task is to widen the trails blazed for her—and more. She must build them into great highways for women engineers of the future to travel, free of prejudices and discrimination."

In 1952, Margaret retired from Carrier and traded in her hard hat for a silver tea service, which was presented to her by officers and directors of Carrier. In retirement, she enjoyed having tea with friends at her apartment. Margaret died on December 13, 1971.

In 1996, Margaret Ingels was posthumously inducted into the American Society of Heating, Refrigeration, and Air-Conditioning Engineers (ASHRAE) Hall of Fame.

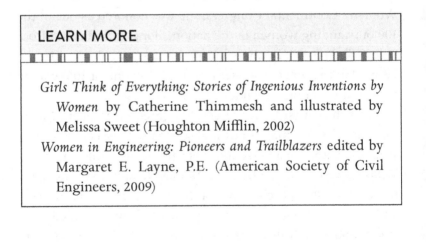

LEARN MORE

Girls Think of Everything: Stories of Ingenious Inventions by Women by Catherine Thimmesh and illustrated by Melissa Sweet (Houghton Mifflin, 2002)

Women in Engineering: Pioneers and Trailblazers edited by Margaret E. Layne, P.E. (American Society of Civil Engineers, 2009)

RUTH GORDON SCHNAPP

Making Buildings Safe

Unlike many students, Ruth Gordon Schnapp loved solving math problems and savored her math homework. In a 2006 interview for the Society of Women Engineers, Ruth explained, "In college, I saved my math homework for dessert, because that was the most fun." Her passion for math led her to embark on a structural engineering career that included building safer schools and hospitals.

Ruth's father, Solomon Gordon, immigrated to America from Lithuania in 1900. After working his way across Europe to Scotland, he boarded a ship for the long trip across the Atlantic Ocean. Finally in America, Gordon sent word to his fiancée, Lea Yoffe, who was waiting in Lithuania. Lea soon joined him,

Ruth Gordon Schnapp in 1984.
Courtesy of the Schnapp Family

> "In college, I saved my math homework for dessert, because that was the most fun."

and the newlyweds eventually settled in Dallas, where Gordon worked as a candy maker. Eight years later, Ruth's older sister, Clara, was born. The family moved to Seattle when Clara was 10 years old, and 8 years after that, Ruth was born on September 19, 1926.

Ruth excelled in school. While in first grade, a teacher coached Ruth in English and math during lunch hours. This allowed Ruth to skip the remainder of the school year and advance to second grade. Ruth also skipped seventh grade, so she entered Queen Anne High School when she was just 12 years old. She loved math, music, and Latin classes. The country was in the midst of World War II, and the government needed people who were good at math and physics. Ruth was placed in an experimental advanced math class in which she studied trigonometry, algebra, and statistics. These special studies fueled Ruth's interest in math.

Ruth's other love was piano, and she played with the choir and orchestra all through high school. At her graduation, in a huge auditorium, she played George Gershwin's "Rhapsody in Blue," accompanied by the orchestra. After the performance, she dreamed of becoming a concert pianist. But, as she explained in 2009, her parents warned her that "you never can tell what's going to happen. You have to study something for which you can make a living."

In 1942, society typically told young girls they should be preparing themselves for marriage and having children, not thinking about how to support a family, so Ruth's parents were unique. "At that time, it was very unusual for a man to believe that women should be treated equally as men and have a higher education. Especially a man like my father, a streetcar man," Ruth explained. She thought, *Well, I better do something else. I'll be an engineer. I have no idea what they do, but I know that they use math.*

Ruth's mom ran into a friend who told her that her son had just received a scholarship to MIT. Ruth's mom suggested that Ruth apply for scholarships too. Ruth applied to MIT, Purdue, and Stanford—all well known for their engineering programs. "When I wrote to Stanford, I didn't even know where it was," she explained. "When they accepted me, I had to find out where it was. I was required to take the Stanford-Binet IQ test and got number one on it."

During the summer breaks when Ruth returned to Seattle, she worked for the aerospace and defense corporation Boeing. Her first year, she was a troubleshooter in the engineering department. Her second summer at Boeing, she worked on changes to the B-17 bomber. Ruth laughed as she recalled her duties, "You laid on the ground on your hands and knees . . . and crawl around in these . . . templates. They were metal, and they had paint on them, and you have to scrape off the paint and then make the change. We worked nine and a half hours a day, hands and feet."

On August 14, 1945, the Japanese surrendered, ending World War II, and Ruth sang in the streets with all the Boeing employees. The next day the Boeing personnel department sent all the women employed in so-called male jobs to take a typing job with the company for lower pay or else quit. Ruth thought that was outrageous. With only four or five weeks left before she went back to school, she became the slowest typist that they ever had—just to spite Boeing and its sexist work practices.

On the first day of classes at Stanford, there were 15 women enrolled. By the second year, only three remained. One day during Ruth's second year at college, she learned of a campus-wide announcement that women had been seen in "inappropriate clothing" below the library. Ruth and two of her female classmates soon discovered they were the offenders. They had to wear jeans to their field classes, which were held late in the afternoon, and they had no time to change into "proper" attire before dinner. Ruth wrote a letter to the editor of the school newspaper, saying, "Well, we're doing forging, foundry, and welding, and if the university wants to pay for our cleaning bills, we'd be glad to change clothes."

The next Monday, posted all over campus and in the daily newspaper was a notice that said that women were to wear appropriate clothes, except for those in certain specified courses.

Ruth was the only women to graduate from Stanford in 1948 with a degree in civil engineering. The other remaining woman in the engineering program graduated with electrical engineering degrees. Before graduation, a professor called them into his office separately. He wanted to know if they were really serious about engineering. After Ruth responded that of course she was serious, he sighed and said, "Well . . . women."

Other male professors were more supportive; they mentored Ruth and helped her to secure scholarships to get into graduate school. There, Ruth did well in civil and industrial engineering. She had heard of civil engineering when she was younger, but she had no idea what civil engineers did. Lillian Gilbreth was in the process of making the profession of industrial engineering well known. But what really interested Ruth were earthquakes, which led her to pursue a master's degree in structural engineering, a division of civil engineering. Structural engineering concentrates on the basic components of a structure, such as beams, columns, beam-column joints, and shear walls. Proper analysis and design of these components are essential to ensuring a bridge or building will be safe and will not collapse in an earthquake.

One night, while Ruth was in graduate school, a friend invited her (along with 22 other classmates) to his parents' house for dinner. It was a very elegant home with a surprising 13 bedrooms and 7 bathrooms. Ruth soon discovered that the house was the very same one in which Lillian Gilbreth, the famous industrial engineer, had grown up! The boy's parents took a liking to Ruth and they became friends. Ruth would stop by the house and visit for a few minutes on her way to classes.

One day, Ruth went around back of the house and noticed a man working under his car. When he stood up, Ruth faced the handsomest man she had ever seen. After a few months of dating, he suggested that they fly to Reno and get married. When Ruth told her friend (the owner of the house) about the plan, her friend insisted that they be married in her house instead. So, Ruth and Michael Schnapp were married in Lillian Gilbreth's old house.

When Ruth began looking for a job, she soon learned to use only her initials on applications because employers never responded when she used her first name, which exposed her as a woman. At several companies, secretaries flat-out told her as she walked in the door, "We don't hire women engineers." Finally, Isadore Thompson, head of a San Francisco structural engineering office, hired Ruth. He told her that he didn't care if she was green, just so long as she could do the job.

Ruth was hired on a Friday, and she was asked to start that Monday to work on building a hospital in Southern California. This hospital incorporated the new technology of welded fastenings, in which the metal is melted during building construction to produce a stronger and more reliable joint or connection. When she returned home that night, Ruth complained to her husband that she didn't know anything about welding.

Relieving her fears and showing his support, Michael reassured Ruth that they had all weekend to learn.

That first job with Isadore Thompson was an important stepping stone for Ruth that led to work at other engineering firms in both design and construction, including the Bechtel Corporation. While at Bechtel, Ruth noticed that male engineers hired after her with exactly the same credentials were paid more than her. When she asked her (male) boss about this, he explained that those men had families to support (as if she didn't), and that her career was somehow optional.

Ruth noted other instances of discrimination against women: "One of my friends—she was the first woman civil engineer— got a job with an oil company," she recalled. "And at that time, men were given automobiles to go from the office to the place where they were working. Well, Jessie, she was given a bicycle."

One day at Bechtel, a colleague asked Ruth if she wanted to work for the state of California. The only thing Ruth needed to work for the state was to take the exam to become a state-certified civil engineer; she passed. Ruth worked for the state of California for 29 years, designing and constructing school buildings to make them more resistant to earthquakes. Ruth had to be constantly creative to construct safe buildings in ways that blended with the architecture. Speaking in 2009, she said, "I was in charge. They might have hated it, but they had to be nice to me." She also insisted her crews fix all structural problems to existing buildings, to bring them into compliance with current building codes.

Six years after receiving her civil engineering license, Ruth decided to try for her structural engineering license. To qualify for that license, one must already be a licensed civil engineer, have worked for a minimum of three years under the supervision of a licensed structural engineer, and pass a grueling

16-hour exam. Only 25 percent of candidates pass the first time they take the exam.

The night before the test, Ruth was awake all night taking care of her son, Michael, who had a temperature of 104 degrees. In a 2006 interview, Ruth explained how she felt after the test, "I don't think I passed. I was kind of sleepy. I didn't know if I have the energy to do it again. It was so tough!" Ruth passed the test and in doing so became the first woman licensed structural engineer in the state of California. It would be another 20 years before another woman would pass that same exam.

"I really loved structural engineering," Ruth said, "especially out in the field." Her position required that she travel a seven-county, 200-mile-radius area of Southern California, checking every public school, hospital, or any construction or reconstruction. Some of Ruth's more high-profile projects were the San Francisco Public Library, San Francisco Asian Art Museum, San Quentin Prison, Palace of the Legion of Honor, San Francisco General Hospital, and the Marin General Hospital.

"It's a very rewarding profession because you know that you're doing something for humanity, because engineering deals with safety. Every branch of engineering deals with safety."

In the 2006 interview, Ruth recounted how one day a crusty old construction superintendent told her that he liked working with her, because when he would ask her a question, she would answer. Apparently, the guy who worked the job before her didn't. With that approval, Ruth said, she knew, "I've made it! I've made it!"

Ruth had avid interests outside of math and engineering. When she and Mike first married, they both agreed that they loved boats, bought a 26-foot-long sailboat, and started racing. When Mike was recalled to active duty during the Korean War, Ruth became skipper. No men wanted to race on her boat, so she assembled a team of women. Every day after work, the women would practice, back and forth through the marina. On race day, there was a lot of press about the "all-girl" sail team, which sailed past two all-male crews.

Due to her commitment to the sport for over 40 years, in 2001 Ruth received the Yachtsman of the Year Award from the Pacific Inter-Club Yacht Association. Ruth, always going back to her engineering, jokingly pointed out that her sailboat was constructed in accordance with the same regulations as the Earthquake Safety for the Public School Buildings.

Ruth summed up her feelings about her work in the 2006 interview. "It's a very rewarding profession because you know that you're doing something for humanity, because engineering deals with safety," she said. "Every branch of engineering deals with safety." Ruth has talked to students at a long list of schools. When guest speaking in 2009, she said, "I became very much interested in helping women and encouraging women to be sure to study math and science, because you never can tell when you're going to need it."

During her retirement, Ruth lived in San Francisco with her three children and grandchildren, and she enjoyed knitting sweaters for her whole crew. She died on January 1, 2014, at the age of 87.

LEARN MORE

The Art of Construction: Projects and Principles for Beginning Engineers & Architects by Mario Salvadori (Chicago Review Press, 2000)

Changing Our World: True Stories of Women Engineers by Sybil E. Hatch (American Society of Civil Engineers, 2006)

Civil Engineering and the Science of Structures (Engineering in Action) by Andrew Solway (Crabtree Publishing, 2012)

JUDITH NITSCH

Engineering Girl

In many ways Judy Nitsch was an average American girl. Growing up in the small town of Southwick, Massachusetts (pop. 5,000), she played softball, was a Girl Scout, took piano lessons, and helped her dad manage a Little League team. Judy also loved to read.

"I can remember that I often asked my parents to drive me to the library right before it closed," she says, "so I could return my books and take out new ones—and the thing I am amazed at is that my parents always took the time to drive me there."

Those supportive parents were Dot and Ed Nitsch. Dot was head nurse at the local hospital, and Ed was a pharmaceutical salesman. Judy was born in the 1950s, the second-oldest child, with an older sister and five younger brothers.

Judith Nitsch.
Courtesy of Worcester Polytechnic Institute

The Nitsch family loved to play cards, especially a game called Setback. Judy recalled, "My sister was always partners with my mom, and my dad got me. They didn't treat us like kids when we played—they were serious, and we had to be also. It was a lot of fun too! They taught us strategy, counting, and quick decisions as we played. I often wonder what influence that had on my ability to do math and solve problems—a lot, I would think!"

On Saturdays, the Nitsch family always had chores. Judy said, "My sister would always choose to watch our three littlest brothers and I would usually take jobs like washing the car, ironing, or washing the kitchen floor. They were tasks that had a start and an end, and you could see what you accomplished. Makes you realize why I became an engineer and my sister is a fabulous kindergarten teacher!"

In sixth grade, Judy was one of 10 children in a special after-school class on advanced math concepts, which was taught by the school principal. In junior high, she was in a special chemistry lab class that involved writing hypotheses, doing experiments, and documenting the results in lab reports. Judy remembered "bumping a lit Bunsen burner during one experiment and setting the desktop on fire!"

After reading that Yale University was going coed in 1969, Judy announced to her mother that she would go to Yale one day. She explained, "She totally encouraged it! I'm the second of seven kids, so I knew my parents couldn't afford it, but I can recall how pleased I was with her reaction."

In high school, Judy had the same math teacher for three years, and he had a lasting impact on her. Judy explained, "Mr. Perry didn't differentiate between the girls and the boys regarding their abilities—he wanted to teach math to whoever wanted to learn it! He bought four Wang desktop calculators for his room—a real unusual investment for a small high school. We thought they were fabulous and we were in heaven using them!"

Judy's favorite class was geometry, and because it was a small school there weren't many advanced math classes such as calculus. She also liked to doodle house plans. When Judy was a junior, she had another chat with her mom about colleges. When Judy told her that she was thinking about attending a state college because of the cost of the Ivy Leagues, her mother got mad and said, "You figure out what school you want to go to, and if we can't afford it, then you look at your second choice. Don't choose your college on what you think we can afford!"

In 1971 Judy graduated as class valedictorian from a class of 119 students at Southwick High School in Massachusetts. She enrolled in Worcester Polytechnic Institute that fall. She said, "I started out as a math major but knew that I'd be switching my major. Math majors either became teachers, which I knew I didn't want to do; became actuaries, which I didn't have the personality for; or went into computer science, and I did not like the Fortran programming course I took during my first semester freshman year."

Judy stood in the middle of the college campus and looked at the different engineering buildings while she was trying to decide. Observing the mechanical engineering building first, she said, "I thought mechanical engineers designed knobs on televisions, so I didn't want to do that. I wasn't keen on my chemistry course as a freshman, so I rejected chemical engineering. I was taking a physics course called Electricity and Magnetism, which I wasn't acing, so I rejected electrical engineering. The next building was the civil engineering building, and I picked it as my major."

During the summer break in college, she worked for Sanderson & Washburn, an engineering and land surveying firm in Connecticut. Judy explained, "They had about 15 employees, and I worked as a drafter in the office. This was 1973, and the owner of the company did not allow the girls that were in the engineering department to work on job sites. We were only allowed to work in the office. And working there for two summers I was only allowed to go out on a construction site once. That's because it was an emergency; something had to get checked because something was due to a client that afternoon. So that was the only time I was allowed to go out on a job site."

Judy learned that the male college students working those summers were only allowed to work in survey crews and be on construction sites. They resented the fact that they didn't get the office and computer experience that she got. They were just as disappointed by the arrangement as Judy was.

Judy graduated from Worcester Polytechnic Institute in 1975 with a bachelor of science degree in civil engineering. First hired at the Framingham, Massachusetts, office of Schofield Brothers Inc., she was the only woman engineer in the firm, beating out 10 men because she had two years of summer job experience. They almost didn't hire her because of her lack of experience on-site. "They wondered if I could use a chain saw and they wondered if I could handle working with the men on job sites," she recalled. "They didn't realize that I have five younger brothers."

> "They wondered if I could use a chain saw and they wondered if I could handle working with the men on job sites. They didn't realize that I have five younger brothers."

Her first job was to widen Wellesley Street in Weston, Massachusetts. The task required designing sidewalks and drainage, as well as lowering the hill to make it safer for drivers and pedestrians. One day while inspecting the construction, Judy parked her car at the bottom of the hill because the road was closed, and a policeman told her to move her car. Judy says, "As I explained why I was there, he didn't believe me and insisted that I move my car. At that point, the contractor saw me and yelled, 'Hey, Judy, come on up here!' so the cop let me through. He didn't expect that a woman would be an engineer, but he especially didn't expect someone 22 years old would be doing this kind of work!"

After three years, Judy was promoted to branch manager. When she passed the national exam and became a professional engineer, she became the firm's first woman vice president. At just 26 she joined the firm's board of directors. In 1982, Judy joined the firm of Allen & Demurjian, and two years later she became a stockholder in the company. The firm was then renamed Allen, Demujrian, Major & Nitsch.

In 1975, Judy was asked to serve on a committee of the Boston Society of Civil Engineers Section (BSCES) of ASCE to plan the national convention. When she went to the first planning meeting, she found that she was the only woman engineer. The other women were engineers' wives, who had come to plan the program for the spouses. She eventually chaired several BSCES committees and was asked to run for the board of directors, which led to her eventually becoming their first female and youngest-ever president.

During this time, she also did graduate work toward a master's degree in civil engineering. In 1982, she received the Society of Women Engineers' Distinguished New Engineer Award.

After Judy and her business partners sold Allen, Demurjian, Major & Nitsch, she decided to open her own firm in 1989. Centered in Boston, the firm grew quickly. In 1996, the company earned a ranking of #172 on the *Inc.* 500, the list of the fastest-growing privately held companies in the United States. Legislation at the time allocated 5 percent of federal contract dollars to women-owned businesses, and with the firm's status as a woman-owned business, Judy won numerous public contracts in the early 1990s. Despite the possibility of increased business opportunities, though legally she was still a women-owned company, Judy changed the company name to Nitsch Engineering in 2006, dropping her first name off. She explains, "We didn't want to be known as a good *woman-owned* engineering firm. We wanted to be known as a good engineering and land surveying firm."

Currently, Nitsch Engineering provides civil engineering, land surveying, traffic engineering, and planning services, as well as GIS (geographical information services) to clients up and down the East Coast, in 18 states and six countries. It does site development projects—parking lots, roads, drainage, sewer, and water system designs. An architect does the building design, and Nitsch Engineering designs the site.

Judy met her husband, Tony Magliozzi, when they were working on a bank project together. Judy explains, "Tony was the project manager for the architectural firm and I was the project manager for the civil engineering aspects of the project. It was 'hate at first sight' for me. But as we worked on the project, I gradually got to like him, and he asked me out after my last construction visit. I said yes."

Judy says she gets her drive from visiting famous architectural marvels: "I would always drag my husband to visit buildings by my architecture clients, like buildings by Frank Gehry. I would also make sure that we visited Frank Lloyd Wright buildings and Santiago Calatrava structures if we were in the area." Sadly, Tony passed away in 2012.

The green roof at Worcester Polytechnic Institute.
Alfredo DiMauro, WPI, Assistant Vice President for Facilities, WPI

One of the highlights of Judy's career was chairing the Board of Trustees Facilities Committee at her alma mater, Worcester Polytechnic Institute, for 16 years. She helped guide the school through several major facilities projects. Judy and Tony contributed to WPI's East Residence Hall's green roof. The roof not only provides thermal insulation, but also implements a storm-water monitoring system to measure the amount and quality of runoff controlled by the green roof. One-third of the roof is planted with sedums (a large flowering plant) that provide students and faculty with opportunities to study the storm water benefits of such roofs. The green roof was the last step needed to make the building LEED certified, a national rating for high-performance, sustainable buildings.

Judy's company implements green techniques into its projects, and is in the forefront of sustainable design. She works with world-renowned architects in the United States and throughout the world. Some of her firm's projects include the New England Aquarium, Brooklyn Bridge Park, the Connecticut Science Center, Boston's Big Dig, the Princeton University Campus Plan, Acadia National Park, and the award-winning MetroWest Water Supply Tunnel project.

About her company, she said, "About one-third of Nitsch Engineering's engineers are women—compared with 10 percent nationally. We look for the best-qualified candidates of both genders, but I think women seek us out because they see women at all levels of our firm, including three women engineers as shareholders. They realize they would have a good opportunity to get ahead without discrimination."

> "We look for the best-qualified candidates of both genders, but I think women seek us out because they see women at all levels of our firm, including three women engineers as shareholders."

Judy helps other women engineers through her participation in many organizations, including the Society of Women Engineers. Nitsch Engineering organizes Boston's annual Introduce a Girl to Engineering Day. She said, "I will speak with any woman engineer who calls asking for career advice, because as a young engineer I had no women to talk with professionally. For the first eight years of my career, I was the only woman engineer at my workplace."

She tells young girls, "Remember, all of the rookies—male or female—on every construction site get teased and embarrassed by the old-timers. And usually the newbie is asked to get coffee. That's just a rite of passage. Being the only woman

GREEN ARCHITECTURE, ENGINEERING, AND SUSTAINABILITY

As we build for the future, architects, engineers, and landscape architects face challenges in the sustainability of our current lifestyles and environments. These architects and engineers must pay attention to critical global environmental issues such as energy, pollution, transportation, agriculture, land use, construction, water access and use, and ecological destruction.

LEED (Leadership in Energy and Environmental Design) is an internationally recognized green building program, which can be applied to individual buildings and homes as well as to entire neighborhoods and communities. LEED certification for commercial buildings and neighborhoods must satisfy all LEED prerequisites and earn a minimum of 40 points on a 110-point LEED rating system scale. Currently 135 countries around the world have LEED-certified projects. Among these prerequisites are:

➤ Sustainable energy use in heating, ventilation, and cooling systems. Examples: efficient insulation, window placement.

➤ Renewable energy generation through solar panels, wind tunnels, water solar heating, and heat pumps.

➤ Sustainable building incorporating reusable building materials and low-volatile organic compounds.

➤ Waste management on the property, even during construction. Examples: use of gray water for gardens and sewage-reducing toilets.

➤ Building placement that works with the surrounding environment.

is sometimes lonely, and often enlightening, but being female helps folks remember you."

With more than 35 years of engineering experience, Judy is a registered professional engineer in 21 states. She has received many prestigious awards, including the American

"Remember, all of the rookies—male or female—on every construction site get teased and embarrassed by the old-timers. And usually the newbie is asked to get coffee. That's just a rite of passage."

Society of Civil Engineers' Parcel-Sverdrup Engineering Management Award, the Boston Society of Architects' Women in Design Award, the Patriots Trail Girl Scout Council's Leading Women Award, and the Women's Transportation Seminar Boston Chapter's Woman of the Year Award.

On June 19, 2010, Judy was awarded an honorary doctor of science degree by the Massachusetts Maritime Academy at its

LISA BROTHERS

In 2011, Lisa Brothers was named president and chief executive officer at Nitsch Engineering. Her 29 years in design, construction, and management of roadways; site development; sustainable design; and infrastructure-related projects began when Lisa first heard about engineering from her typing teacher in high school. Her teacher knew that Lisa was good at math and science and asked, "What about engineering?" Judy now serves as founding principal and chairman of the board, and continues to work full-time, focusing on client relations and business development.

167th commencement, recognizing Judy for her contributions to the engineering field and her efforts to encourage others to pursue engineering careers.

Judy said, "Oh, I love what I do, no doubt about it. The thing I like about engineering—and civil engineering in particular—is that it is tangible. I can drive down roads I designed. I go into shopping centers and office parks that I know the building is there because I put it there."

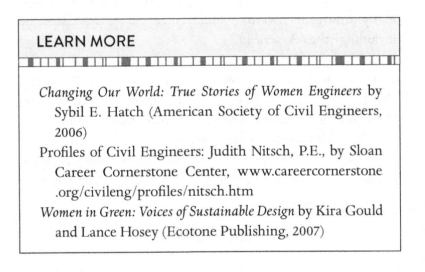

LEARN MORE

Changing Our World: True Stories of Women Engineers by Sybil E. Hatch (American Society of Civil Engineers, 2006)

Profiles of Civil Engineers: Judith Nitsch, P.E., by Sloan Career Cornerstone Center, www.careercornerstone .org/civileng/profiles/nitsch.htm

Women in Green: Voices of Sustainable Design by Kira Gould and Lance Hosey (Ecotone Publishing, 2007)

AINE BRAZIL

Building Towers

"I think I've always had an affinity for just physically putting things together, even going back to being a child building with Legos," said Aine Brazil, vice chairman of the engineering firm Thornton Tomasetti, in a 2011 *Irish Echo* article. These days, with the responsibility of being in charge of some of New York City's biggest skyscrapers, her building blocks are a lot larger.

Aine Maire Brazil was born on June 9, 1956, in Salthill, near Galway, in Ireland. She attended Salerno, a Catholic high school for girls about which she recalled, "It was a small school with only 120 students and I had a math teacher who came in on Saturday mornings to teach the three girls in my class who wanted to do higher-level math. She gave up her Saturday morning to come in and teach us. The school also provided for me a teacher for physics and chemistry—I was the only one in the class—so that I could prepare to study the engineering." Aine admitted that, at the time, she didn't really know what an engineer did.

Growing up, Aine always felt like she had an aptitude for math and the sciences. She noted, "There was recognition in our school that you should really be given the opportunity to pursue whatever career you wanted. My parents were the same. They felt there were no boundaries, and I came to college with that thought."

When Aine enrolled in an engineering course at University College in Galway, she was one of only three women among the 60 students in the class. She graduated in 1977 with a bachelor of science degree in engineering. While working toward her master's degree at the Imperial College of Science and Technology in London, Aine was the only woman in her class of 20 students.

When Aine graduated there were few jobs in Ireland, so she moved to London to work with the building firm Arup. There she stayed for five years before moving back to Dublin when the economy picked up. In 1982, she moved to New York. Her boyfriend, also a structural engineer, who is now her husband, wanted to gain experience in the United States, where he was born. They had planned to stay only two years, but that soon changed. Aine explained, "I wanted to spend a couple of years there to get broader experience. I didn't intend to immigrate and stay in the US. However, when I arrived in New York, I discovered that it was just a fantastic city for a structural engineer to work in. It's the center for a lot of work done around the United States but also around the world. I enjoyed living here, but I think the work was the major contributor in deciding to stay."

Aine joined a 45-person engineering firm, Lev Zetlin, and immediately was working overtime her first weekend. The firm eventually changed its name to Thornton Tomasetti and the company now employs over 700 people, making it one of the largest structural engineering firms in the world. Aine was appointed the company's vice chairman in April 2012.

With a 30-year career with Thornton Tomasetti, Aine has led structural engineering design projects for many high-rise buildings, most of them in New York City's Times Square area, such as the 40-story skyscraper Eleven Times Square, but also across the country and the world, including Oklahoma's tallest building, the Devon Tower in Oklahoma City, and Soyak Tower in Istanbul, Turkey.

Structural engineers have received more attention since the 9/11 tragedy at the World Trade Center in New York City. The unique design of the skeletal structures prevented the total collapse of the buildings initially and the possible deaths of thousands more people. "I think after September 11, people understand a little better that there's a skeleton in each building for which the structural engineer is responsible," Aine said, musing on the tragedy. "Very few buildings, if any, would have withstood that sort of impact, for as long. Those planes probably sliced through some of the interior columns as well as more than half the exterior columns [on the impacted side], and most buildings would have come down right away. But that design stood up long enough that it probably saved 15,000 lives."

Recalling standout projects in her career thus far, Aine feels that New York Hospital was one of the more challenging and innovative. "The campus has been in existence since the early 1900s," she said, "and was built on lots of pieces of land around 68th and 71st Streets on the east side of Manhattan—but there was almost no land available in the area since the early '60s. The only way to find land to develop critical new buildings was up and over the Franklin D. Roosevelt highway."

Aine was referring to the fact that the hospital abuts the East River and a six-lane highway beside the river, so major construction work was tricky. "I was there at midnight on a Saturday night when they lifted that first major truss section over the highway using the 1,000-ton crane barge," she recalled. "They were inches away from the walls of the psychiatric hospital. These pieces were built in New Jersey, 95 feet wide, three trusses together with the frame, so it was 50 feet long. These seven major segments were lifted into place and they did it at night, reopening the highway by six in the morning. Closures were permitted only for about five or six hours."

> "There's a certain amount of whistling. I don't perceive it as sexual harassment, but simply a leftover 'tradition' in a male-dominated industry."

Early in her career, Aine had to fight for the respect of men out in the field. At a job site in North Carolina, she said, male contractors listened to her politely but ignored her demands. "I was being 'yes, ma'amed,' but then they wouldn't do what I told them, and I had to go back and get them to fix the problem. Eventually you find a way to gain their respect by showing your knowledge and understanding of the construction process."

These days, when she has to go out into the field to inspect foundations, steel columns, and roof beams, Aine carefully walks across scaffolds high above the ground. Some of the workers on the buildings are surprised to see a woman under the hard hat. Aine says, "There's a certain amount of whistling.

Aine Brazil and the Thornton Tomasetti team responsible for structural engineering of the Johns Hopkins Hospital New Clinical Building, the country's largest single-facility health care construction project.
©John Madere

I don't perceive it as sexual harassment, but simply a leftover 'tradition' in a male-dominated industry."

Aine still speaks with a touch of an Irish accent despite 20 years in the United States. She doesn't mind standing out in a profession that is still male-dominated. "One thing about the industry here in New York is, if you're a woman, people will remember you," she has said. "In any business it's not a bad thing to be remembered, so long as it's not for the wrong reasons." Reaching to ever-greater heights, Aine is currently working on designing the Hudson Yards development in New York City on the west side of Manhattan that will cover six city blocks over old rail yards—once again, a Manhattan solution to "creating land."

LEARN MORE

The Big Dig: Reshaping an American City by Peter Vander-
  warker (Little, Brown Young Readers, 2001)
Changing Our World: True Stories of Women Engineers by
  Sybil E. Hatch (American Society of Civil Engineers,
  2006)
Engineering the City: How Infrastructure Works by Matthys
  Levy and Richard Panchyk (Chicago Review Press,
  2000)

PART THREE

LANDSCAPE ARCHITECTS

SCOTTISH GENTLEMAN Gilbert Laing Meason first used the term "landscape architecture" in his book *On the Landscape Architecture of the Great Painters of Italy*, published in 1828. Meason wrote about the relationship between architecture and landscape—built form with natural form. Nineteenth-century landscape designers Frederick Law Olmsted and Calvert Vaux used the term in their winning entry for the design of Central Park in New York City. In 1863, they each gave themselves the title of landscape architect: someone with the professional skill of designing with plantings, landform, water, paving, and other structures.

Then in 1893, architecture critic Mariana Van Rensselaer brought the garden to new recognition and described the landscape architect as "a gardener, an engineer, and an artist, who like an architect considers beauty and utility together."

The first landscape architecture degrees were offered in 1900 at MIT; the program diverged from MIT's architecture program in the second year of study. Headed by Boston architect Guy

Lowell, the program had 10 students in its first year. Martha Brookes Hutcheson entered the program in 1900. Right behind her was Marian Coffin, who became the first woman graduate from the program, in 1904. Harvard also started a landscape architecture department in 1900, but they didn't start accepting women until 1942.

Marian Coffin outlined the struggles of being a woman landscape architect around the turn of the 19th century thusly: "Unless a woman has capital or influence, or is able to get into a good office, she is very foolish to take up the profession as a means of support. It is hard to get a start, as there is a prejudice in many offices against employing women. . . . A woman has to solve many problems and learn the ropes entirely by herself, while a man has the advantage of long office training and experience."

Despite this hardship, Guy Lowell felt women were in fact a better fit than men in the garden, explaining, "A woman will fuss with a garden in a way that no man will ever have the patience to do. If necessary, she will sit on a campstool and see every individual plant into the ground. I have no hesitation in saying that where the relatively small garden is concerned, the average woman will do better than the average man."

Women landscape architects were historically more accepted than women architects. Historian Deborah Nevins explained, "In terms of fame and influence in their time, women landscape architects were far ahead of their sisters in architecture, no doubt in part because women and gardening, as opposed to women and building, were naturally connected in the public mind. It was all right to give a woman a commission for a garden but women were not supposed to know anything about construction. Moreover, a building involves more money than a garden, and our society traditionally has been reluctant to allow

AMERICA'S BEST LANDSCAPE ARCHITECTURE PROGRAMS

In 2013, *DesignIntelligence* ranked the top 10 architectural design schools in the United States based on surveys and interviews by students, deans, and design professionals. There are more than 60 accredited and candidacy landscape architecture programs in the United States.

Top 10 Undergraduate Landscape Architecture Programs
1. Louisiana State University
2. Virginia Polytechnic Institute and State University
3. Pennsylvania State University
4. Kansas State University
5. Texas A&M University
6. Cornell University
7. California Polytechnic State University, San Luis Obispo
8. Purdue University
9. University of Georgia
10. Ball State University

Top 10 Graduate Landscape Architecture Programs
1. Harvard University
2. Virginia Polytechnic Institute and State University
3. Cornell University
4. Louisiana State University
5. University of Virginia
6. University of Pennsylvania
7. Pennsylvania State University
8. Rhode Island School of Design
9. Texas A&M University
10. University of California, Berkeley

women to spend large sums of someone else's money to exercise creativity."

Landscape architecture has greatly expanded since its inception; it now consists of planning and designing the grounds in and around parks, playgrounds, zoos, skate parks, residences, campuses, shopping centers, gardens, golf courses, and recreation areas for parks, recreational facilities, highways, airports, and other properties. Landscape architecture may incorporate the areas of botany, horticulture, the fine arts, architecture, industrial design, engineering, geology and the earth sciences, environmental psychology, geography, and ecology.

In 1977, the student body in Harvard's landscape architecture program was 50 percent women. Today, it's 70 percent women. Though that percentage is higher than for architecture and engineering, challenges for women in the field still exist, especially in getting positions teaching at colleges and universities.

Yet as the women highlighted in these pages prove beyond a doubt, girls can play in the dirt just as well as boys.

BEATRIX FARRAND

Planting Seeds

Renowned American author Henry James called Beatrix Farrand "dear brave Trix" after she became the first woman to break into the male-dominated landscape architecture field, going on to have a 50-year career and more than 200 commissions.

Beatrix Cadwalader Jones was born on June 19, 1872, in a New York City townhouse. When she was just three weeks old, her parents took her to her grandparents' summer home named Pencraig, in Newport, Rhode Island, the summer resort town where New York high society went to escape the city's heat. A week later, she became so seriously ill that her parents had her quickly baptized in case she died.

Beatrix Farrand and Cubby, 1934.
Beatrix Farrand Society Archives

As a young girl, Beatrix loved to trot through the gardens of her grandparents' estate with her young aunt, Edith Jones, who would become known as the novelist Edith Wharton and Beatrix's lifelong supporter. When Beatrix was four years old, as she ran through the gardens at Pencraig, her grandmother Lucretia taught her the names of the flowers, as well as how to cut off the dead blooms. Beatrix spoke of the fashionable roses of the day—with names like Baroness Rothchild, Marie Van Houtte, and Bon Silent—as if they were her playground friends.

Beatrix was the only child of Minnie and Freddy Jones. Minnie's great-grandfather was General John Cadwalader, a Revolutionary War hero. Freddy's great-great-grandfather, General Ebenezer Stevens, helped to tip the tea into Boston Harbor during the Boston Tea Party of 1773. He was also known for having "the best garden in old New York." Beatrix's grandmother Lucretia had the first espaliered, or trellised, fruit garden in Newport. In fact, five generations of Beatrix's family were gardeners.

As was the norm for a young lady of high society in Victorian New York City, Beatrix was privately tutored in French, German, Italian, and Greek. She enjoyed reading and the arts and considered a career in music, though she remained fascinated by flowers and nature.

When Beatrix was seven, her father took the family to Bar Harbor, Maine, for the first time. Beatrix's grandparents had already started taking summer retreats to Bar Harbor, nicknamed "Philadelphia by the sea." Beatrix would watch her mother Minnie lay out the gardens and grounds at Reef Point, the name of the estate that they had built. Meanwhile, Beatrix would explore the woods and transplant plants to the gardens.

When Beatrix was 10 years old, she experienced a family crisis. Her father left the family and moved to Paris with his mistress—though Beatrix's parents didn't officially divorce until she was 24 years old. Despite the dramatic breakup, Beatrix's mother remained close friends with her sister-in-law, Edith Wharton, and served as her literary agent for many years.

Always fascinated with plants, Beatrix's interest in landscape architecture was sparked by the words of her friend Mariana Van Rensselaer, who said, "A landscape gardener is a gardener, an engineer, and an artist who, like an architect, considers beauty and utility together." Her mother's cousin John Cadwalader said, "Let her be a gardener or, for that matter, anything she wants to be. What she wishes to do will be well done."

Beatrix's real introduction to landscape design came in 1893, when she studied under Charles Sprague Sargent, the first director of the Arnold Arboretum in Boston. She wrote, "Possibly what first led me to think seriously of landscape gardening was a trip to the World's Fair, taken in company with Prof. and Mrs. Sargent of Boston."

Professor Sargent opened up the world of the Arnold Arboretum for Beatrix to study. She also traveled to Europe and studied the gardens of England, France, Italy, and Algiers. She traveled with her Aunt Edith, who wrote about the fundamentals of formal garden design in her book *Italian Villas and Their Gardens.*

In 1896, at the age of 23, Beatrix set up a design office on the top floor of the home she shared with her mother in New York City. Since she was a member of high society, she used her social connections to find work, and she was soon creating gardens for clients with estates in Newport, the Berkshires, and Maine. In 1899, Beatrix was the only woman in the group of 11 founders of the American Society of Landscape Architects (ASLA).

In 1912, Beatrix was commissioned by Princeton University to plan the grounds of its new Graduate College. She designed a plan for the entire campus and became the consulting landscape architect for the university. For more than 30 years, she was in charge of the campus grounds. She had such a presence on campus that students lovingly called her "the bush woman"—even though Beatrix favored vines over bushes. She also supervised the Yale University grounds for 23 years and the University of Chicago grounds for 14 years. She additionally helped create campus grounds for Oberlin College, Vassar College, Hamilton College, the California Institute of Technology, and acted as an advisor for the Arnold Arboretum of Harvard University.

Beatrix created the professional model for other landscape practices to follow. Her work in the field combined the craft of gardening, the science of plants, and the art of design. Ellen

ELIZABETH J. BULLARD

Elizabeth Bullard first began working in landscape architecture as an assistant to her father, Oliver Bullard, who worked alongside celebrated landscaper Frederick Law Olmsted Sr. When her father died suddenly in 1890, the Bridgefield, Connecticut, city council offered Elizabeth her father's position as superintendent of their city park. Olmsted not only highly recommended Elizabeth for the job, he also proposed they give her more authority due to the struggles that she would face as a woman. Elizabeth turned down the job fearing rivalries from male landscape designers; instead she created her own architectural design practice. A landscaping job for Smith College in Northampton, Massachusetts, was one project that she designed through her own practice, working with Olmsted's office. Elizabeth was the second female member of the American Society of Landscape Architects and was made a fellow in 1899.

Biddle Shipman and Marian Cruger Coffin both based their practices on Beatrix's model.

The first step in Beatrix's design process was to sit down with her clients and discuss their needs and likes. Beatrix felt that a design evolved; the garden was not set in stone by the first drawing. She worked with the gardeners and clients for many years after the projects were completed, attested by her devotion to many years of work on college campuses.

When Woodrow Wilson became president in March 1913, First Lady Ellen Wilson, was making plans for the East and West Gardens of the White House. After reviewing designs made by the US Army Corps of Engineers, which controlled the design of the White House and grounds, Mrs. Wilson requested Beatrix design the gardens instead. Sadly, Ellen Wilson died 17 months later, and the garden plans stopped. When President

White House Southeast Garden, designed by Beatrix Farrand, spring 1921.
Library of Congress LC-J717-X98-51

The Occidental College quad, early 1950s.
Courtesy of Occidental College Special Collections and College Archives

Wilson remarried in 1916, the new Mrs. Wilson, Edith Bolling Galt, approved Beatrix's plans, and the garden was completed.

One evening Beatrix was asked to a dinner at the home of the president of Yale to discuss the campus's garden plan. During dinner, Beatrix met Max Farrand, a Princeton graduate and professor of history at Yale. They were married in 1913; Beatrix was 41 and Max was 44. The newlyweds, named "MaxTrix" by their close friends, lived in New Haven, Connecticut, so Max could be near Yale. In 1924, Max resigned from Yale to spend more time doing research and writing. In 1926, the Farrands moved to Southern California, where Max headed the new Huntington Library in San Marino. Beatrix had a studio built that connected by pergola to the director's house at the Huntington Library.

During the 14 years that the Farrands lived in California, Beatrix traveled back and forth across the country working on projects from the West Coast to Chicago to the East Coast.

Beatrix's largest project in Southern California was the redesign of the Occidental College campus. Charles H. Thorne, son of the founder of Montgomery Ward, donated money to build an auditorium to honor his late wife. The campus needed to be redesigned to incorporate the new building. Thorne was from Chicago, where Beatrix had just designed the University of Chicago campus grounds, and he requested that Beatrix or someone as experienced as her design the landscape at Occidental.

Thorne's vision was to have the new auditorium at the west end of a quadrangle. The east end housed the Clapp Library, a key part of campus. Beatrix created the quad with mature California oak trees, yellow terraces and steps, concrete bench

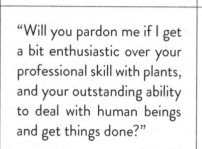

"Will you pardon me if I get a bit enthusiastic over your professional skill with plants, and your outstanding ability to deal with human beings and get things done?"

seats and tables, and teak benches. Beatrix worked with Occidental College for five years, until her husband's retirement from the Huntington Library. Occidental comptroller Fred McLain and Beatrix became friends, and he praised her work, asking, "Will you pardon me if I get a bit enthusiastic over your professional skill with plants, and your outstanding ability to deal with human beings and get things done?"

Beatrix said her work at Occidental "lies very close to my heart." She incorporated olive trees and flowering and native plants "to give the campus real distinction and beauty," and native oaks around campus to "give dignity to the hillsides and charm to any buildings set on them." The beauty of the campus has survived the test of time. Every year Occidental College continues to be ranked in the top 10 on many "most beautiful college campus" lists, most recently in 2012 by *Newsweek* and College Prowler, an online college resource for students.

One project for which Beatrix is particularly well known was also her most challenging and rewarding. Dumbarton Oaks in Washington, DC, was the 53-acre estate of diplomat Robert Woods Bliss and his wife, Mildred Barnes Bliss. When Beatrix started designing the estate grounds, she was almost 50 years old. She continued to work on the project until 1951, when she was 79. Mildred Bliss said about Beatrix's design, "Dumbarton Oaks has its own personality sculpted from Beatrix's knowledge and wisdom and from the daydreams and vision of the owners."

Dumbarton Oaks was a private estate from 1921 to 1940, until Bliss donated the estate and gardens to Harvard to be used as a research center and public garden. Thousands of visitors have toured the site, which has been called one of the most beautiful gardens in America. Coincidentally, in 2005, Venturi Scott Brown and Associates designed an $18 million research library and renovation of the entire Dumbarton property. The *Washington Times* said, "By hiring Mr. Venturi to design the library, Dumbarton Oaks also benefited from the planning and preservation expertise of Ms. Scott Brown to improve its campus, which was in need of a major overhaul."

About her childhood "friends" in her grandmother's garden, Beatrix wrote in *The Garden as a Picture*, "In order to have good gardens we must really care for the plants in them and know them individually as well as collectively. . . . He [the landscape architect] must know intimately the form and texture as well as the colour of all the plants he uses; for plants are to the gardener what his palette is to a painter."

In May 1941, Beatrix and Max both retired and returned to their roots in Reef Point, Maine, where they worked on creating a landscape study center on the property. After Max's death in 1945, Beatrix helped complete one of Max's long-term research projects. With help from the Huntington Library, a restoration of a "fair copy" of *The Autobiography of Benjamin Franklin* was published in 1949. Beatrix sold Reef Point in 1955, and moved to the nearby Garland Farm, where she worked on redesigning the property's garden well into her 80s. She lived there until her death on February 28, 1959, at the age of 87.

LEARN MORE

Beatrix Farrand: Private Gardens, Public Landscapes by Judith Tankard (Monacelli Press, 2009)

Beatrix Farrand's American Landscapes: Her Gardens and Campuses by Diana Balmori, Diane Kostial McGuire, and Eleanor M. McPeck (Sagapress, 2003)

The Collected Writings of Beatrix Farrand: American Landscape Gardener, 1872–1959 by Beatrix Farrand (University Press of New England, 2009)

ELLEN BIDDLE SHIPMAN

Dean of American Landscape Architecture

It's rather surprising that Ellen McGowan Biddle, raised in the Wild West during the 1870s, would eventually be referred to as the "Dean of American Landscape Architecture."

Ellen's father, Colonel James Biddle, was a career military man who fought in the Civil War. Ellen's mother was Ellen Fish McGowen, whose father, John McGowen, was the captain of a Union merchant ship and was in command of the ship when it fired the first shots of the Civil War.

After the Civil War, Colonel Biddle, Ellen, and their two sons, 14-month-old Jack and two-month-old David, moved wherever Colonel Biddle was stationed: first Macon, Georgia, then military outposts in Mobile, Alabama, then 250 miles upriver

Ellen Biddle Shipman in Boston, circa 1890.
Courtesy of Judith B. Tankard, Nancy Angell Streeter Collection

to Natchez, Mississippi. After eventually settling in Brenham, Texas, Ellen's doctor felt that due to her stress and the hot climate, Ellen and the boys should return to her parents' home in Philadelphia for the summer.

Baby Ellen, whom they called "Nellie," was born on November 5, 1869. When Ellen and the boys and Nellie were well enough to travel again, they boarded a train for the seven-day trip from New York City to San Francisco. Colonel Biddle was stationed 500 miles from San Francisco in Camp Halleck, Nevada, where the family lived among the sagebrush for the next two years. The family was uprooted again, first to Fort Riley, Kansas, and then to Fort Lyon, Colorado, where Native Americans were then revolting against the US military's presence.

One spring day, Ellen and the children set out into town to shop. Ellen stopped the mule-driven cart so that the children could pick the new buds that were peeking through the snow. After living in the sagebrush of the desert and then enduring months of snow, the children developed an appreciation for flowers that their mother helped foster. The children were delighted to gather the wildflowers, the verbena in all colors and the little forget-me-nots.

The East Coast newspapers were filled with stories of the Indian uprisings, so Ellen's parents insisted that Ellen and the children return home. On the train ride back east, the children, by now thoroughly accustomed to life on the frontier, were awed by apple trees. Four-year-old Nellie, while passing a cemetery, exclaimed, "Oh! Mama, look at the beautiful stones growing out of there!" At their grandparents' house, they saw their first cultivated garden.

After getting the boys settled at a Connecticut school in December 1875, Ellen and Nellie set off once again—this time to Arizona to rejoin the Colonel. At Fort Whipple in the Arizona territory, Nellie was fearless and strong. She rode horses, played marbles, flew kites, and gathered wildflowers with the other children at the outpost. In Arizona, the Biddle family added another baby boy, Nick, to the family.

When Nellie was 10, her uncle offered to take her back east with him. Her mother felt that it was time for her to attend school regularly and have the companionship of other girls. After the rough trip from Arizona to Los Angeles, where they rendezvoused, her mother wrote in her diary, "My brother said that the little one looked like a young Indian when he met her at Los Angeles, she was so sunburned, covered with dust and dirt, and the waist of her dress torn in shreds. She interested the passengers greatly, telling them of her life in Arizona and her travels."

Back on the East Coast, Ellen, no longer called Nellie, was sent to one of the finest finishing schools, which was run by the granddaughter of Thomas Jefferson. Miss Sarah Randolph's Patapsco Institute in Ellicott City, Maryland, was created not only to provide an excellent education but also to teach refined young ladies how to run a home. Classes consisted of basic housekeeping, sewing, and cooking along with mathematics, science, languages, painting, botany, philosophy, and psychology. The margins of Ellen's notebooks were soon full of drawings of house and garden plans. Miss Sarah, noticing young Ellen's passion, gave her an architectural dictionary as a history prize.

When Ellen turned 18, the Biddle family moved to Washington, DC, where the Colonel worked for the War Department. Ellen kept busy with the social scene in the nation's capital. In her 20s, she shared a house in Massachusetts with friends and enrolled at Radcliffe College, then known as Harvard Annex. Ellen spent a lot of time with her housemate's cousin, Louis

Evan Shipman, a young playwright from a respectable New York family. Louis and Ellen married, moved to Connecticut, and welcomed a daughter the next year, named Ellen, like her mother.

> "As I look back I realize it was at that moment that a garden became for me the most essential part of a home."

The following year, Ellen and Louis moved to Cornish, New Hampshire, a celebrated summer resort town where many artists and writers lived. They found the little artists' colony they shared with painters, sculptors, illustrators, writers, and musicians was perfect for the young couple. At a party the first night in Cornish, Ellen first realized her gardening passion. She reminisced years later, "Just a few feet below, where we stood upon a terrace, was a Sunken Garden with rows bathed in moonlight of white lilies standing as an altar for Ascutney. As I look back I realize it was at that moment that a garden became for me the most essential part of a home. But years of work had to intervene before I could put this belief, born that glorious night, into actual practice."

The inhabitants of the artist colony created extraordinary gardens, and Cornish was described as "the most beautifully gardened village of all America." Ellen designed her first garden there, a country garden with a dirt path lined with summer flowers, which was her model for many other designs.

In 1899, Ellen and Louis stayed in the home of Charles Platt and his wife while their own house was being built. Platt was a landscape painter when he first came to Cornish, but after a trip to Italy, he started designing landscapes and eventually homes incorporating Italian design elements. Ellen, in her spare time, created house plans on the drawing board in Platt's studio.

When Platt saw the drawings, he sent her a note that said, "If you can do as well as I was, you better keep on." As encouragement, he gave Ellen her own drawing board and other tools of the trade, including a T-square for drawing straight lines, and drafting implements.

In 1903, Ellen and Louis purchased Brook Place, a 200-acre property where Ellen designed the architecture, interiors, and landscape. The property became her personal classroom. She explained later, "Working daily in my garden for fifteen years taught me to know plants, their habits and their needs."

Ellen and Louis had two more children, Evan in 1904 and Mary in 1908. Ellen homeschooled her three children and loved it. Two years after Mary's birth, however, Louis left the family

A garden Ellen designed for Henry W. Longfellow Place, Cambridge, Massachusetts.
Library of Congress HABS MASS,9-CAMB,1-30

and ran off to London. Now 41 years old and needing to support herself and her three children, Ellen looked to designing gardens and landscapes as a career.

By that time, Ellen's friend and longtime mentor Charles Platt had a successful business designing architecture and landscapes for the rich and famous from coast to coast. One day, Platt said to Ellen, "I like the outcome of your efforts at Brooks Place. Could you do the planting for the places I am building?" Ellen didn't think that she was an expert at drafting, so Platt had one of his assistants instruct her on landscape drawing. After collaborating with Platt, Ellen soon developed a vast base of clients, creating construction plans for walls, pools, and small garden buildings and working on gardens and estates from New York and Ohio to Michigan and Washington.

In 1920, Ellen moved and opened her own design practice in New York City, where her younger brother Nick ran a successful law office. She purchased and remodeled a four-story townhouse on the corner of Beekman Place and East 50th Street. Her design offices were on the first floor, her home was on the second floor, and two apartments occupied the top two floors. Her townhouse became a place to show off her interior design talents, which soon became the main source of her income.

Ellen's design practice grew through word of mouth, photos of her gardens in magazines, and associations with garden clubs, which were very popular in the early 20th century. Over the years, she had 24 clients in Greenwich, Connecticut; 17 in Mount Kisco, New York; 57 on Long Island; 44 in Grosse Point Shores, Michigan; and 45 in the Cleveland/Toledo, Ohio, area. Houston, Buffalo, and Winston-Salem, North Carolina, were also towns where Ellen had many clients. Ellen's landscape designs graced the estates of captains of industry, financial leaders, and patrons of the arts, including the families of the Fords, Astors, and du Ponts.

Ellen Shipman in her Beekman Place office, New York, 1920s.
Courtesy of Judith B. Tankard, Nancy Angell Street Collection

Ellen hired only women designers, including Beatrix Farrand, also based out of New York City. She mainly employed graduates from Lowthorpe School of Landscape Architecture for Women in Groton, Massachusetts. In the school catalog she is quoted, "There is no profession so suited to women, so needed and so repaying in every way—nor any that at once gives so much of health, wealth, and happiness." When clients walked into Ellen's design offices, they would catch a glimpse of girls in blue smocks bent over drafting boards.

"Until women took up landscaping, gardening in this country was at its lowest ebb."

A strong advocate for women, Ellen pointed out, "Before women took hold of the profession, landscape architects were doing cemetery work. . . . Until women took up landscaping, gardening in this country was at its lowest ebb. The renaissance of the art was due largely to the fact that women, instead of working over their board, used plants as if they were painting pictures, as an artist would. Today women are at the top of their profession."

In 1921, *House and Garden, House Beautiful*, and several other magazines showcased Ellen's gardens and popular collaborations with architects. *House and Garden* praised Ellen in 1933 as the "Dean of Women Landscape Architects." During both world wars, Ellen was an outspoken advocate of the "victory garden." To help in the war effort, families grew fruit, vegetable, and herb gardens for their personal use to help preserve food supplies for the troops. She offered the use of her New York office to the Garden Club of America so it could provide information about victory gardens to the nation.

In 1947, at the age of 78, Ellen closed her office and spent her retirement years living on the island of Bermuda, in a house that she designed. The property had views of both sides of the island and gardens running down the south slope. She died in her home on March 27, 1950.

LEARN MORE

The Garden Club of America: One Hundred Years of a Growing Legacy by William Seale (Smithsonian, 2013)

The Gardens of Ellen Biddle Shipman by Judith B. Tankard (Sagapress, 1996)

A Genius for Place: American Landscapes of the Country Place Era by Robin Karson (University of Massachusetts Press, 2007)

MARIAN CRUGER COFFIN

Covered All Grounds

For more than 53 years, Marian Coffin created the beautiful landscapes of our nation's finest estates. Her design process, which she outlined in her book *Trees and Scrubs for Landscape Effects*, covered the entire property. She mastered the monumental task of creating landscapes for huge estates while sticking to her design philosophy: "Simplicity is beauty's prime ingredient."

Marian Cruger Coffin came from an illustrious East Coast family. She was born in Scarborough, a northern suburb of New York City, on September 27, 1876. Her mother, Alice Church Coffin, was a descendant of Richard Church, one of the passengers on the *Mayflower*. Her father, Julian Ravenel Coffin, had

Marian Cruger Coffin, 1904.
Courtesy of the Winterthur Library: Winter Archives

ancestors who settled the island of Nantucket. Marian's great-great-uncle was the Revolutionary War–era painter John Trumbull, and her uncle Benjamin Church was an engineer who worked with Frederick Law Olmsted on the design of Central Park.

Marian's parents were married in 1874, and Marian was born two years later. When she was seven, her father passed away of complications from malaria. The family was left with just $300 and so lived for several years with the sister of Marian's mother, in Geneva, New York. Marian was a fragile child and went to public school for only a few months. Instead, she was privately tutored at home.

> "I secretly cherished the idea of being a great artist. . . . My desire to create was strong."

Marian's mother, Alice, had high-society friends. When Alice's best friend, Mary Foster, married Colonel Henry A. du Pont, Alice was a bridesmaid. The groom was a member of the du Pont dynasty, one of America's richest and most prominent families in the 19th and 20th centuries. Marian grew up best friends with the du Pont children, Louise and Henry, and played with them on the du Pont estate, Winterthur.

In a 1932 letter Marian lamented, "I secretly cherished the idea of being a great artist . . . but that dream seemed in no way possible of realization. . . . My desire to create was strong, I did not seem to possess talent for music, writing, painting, or sculpture, at that time, the only outlet a woman had to express any artistic ability. . . . My artistic yearning lay fallow until I realized it was necessary to earn my living."

When Marian was 16, her family moved just a few doors down to live with Alice's brother and his wife, Maria, until they moved to Boston so that Marian could go to school. Realizing Marian's quest to add art to her life and earn an income, an architect friend suggested that she try landscape architecture, a new field that was open to women. She entered the landscape architecture program at MIT in 1901, one of only two female students in the program. She said, "You can imagine how terrifying such an institution as 'Tech' appeared to a young woman who had never gone more than a few months to a regular school, and when it was reluctantly dragged from me that I had had only a smattering of algebra and hardly knew the meaning of the word 'geometry' the authorities turned from me in calm contempt."

Evidently, the private tutoring that she received during most of her childhood had not prepared Marian for advanced math concepts. "I was told that I was totally unprepared to take the course and refused admittance. It was owing to his [Professor Chandler's] kindness and also to Professor Sargent's and

MARTHA BROOKES HUTCHESON

Martha Brookes Hutcheson was one year ahead of Marian Cruger Coffin in the landscape architecture program at MIT. Martha's interest in landscape architecture was motivated by a visit to a hospital. She recalled, "One day I saw the grounds of Bellevue Hospital in New York, on which nothing was planted, and was overcome with the terrible waste of opportunity for beauty which was not being given to the hundreds of patients who could see it or go to it, in convalescence." In 1935, Martha was the third woman to be named a fellow in the American Society of Landscape Architects.

Mr. Lowell's encouragement that I persevered and was able by intensive tutoring in mathematics to be admitted as a 'special' student in Landscape Architecture, taking all the technical studies and combining the first two years in one so that I finished in three years."

Marian graduated as a special student in the class of 1904, one of a handful of women to finish the program before it was closed a few years later. Her old friend Henry du Pont studied horticulture at Harvard while Marian was at MIT. They shared a love of plants. For a Christmas gift in 1902, Henry sent Marian the four-volume set of *The Cyclopedia of American Horticulture* by Liberty Bailey. Marian wrote to Henry, "My dear Harry, Bailey arrived Friday night to my great joy. I immediately sat down on the floor and hugged all three volumes at once!" The fourth volume was on its way, not yet delivered.

After graduation, Henry and Marian—accompanied by Marian's mother—traveled to England, Europe, and the Dalmatian Coast on the Adriatic Sea to tour gardens. Upon their return to the States, mother and daughter moved to New York City. Finding no jobs available for women landscape designers, Marian opened her own design office out of their home at the National Arts Club. Marian's first commission on record was for the Sprague Estate in Flushing, New York. She described her client-centered design process in a *Country Life in America* article, saying, "In taking up the problem the first step was to ascertain the wishes of the owners. . . . The design must be in scale not only with the house and the grounds but also with the means and taste of the owner."

She soon received the commission for the 3,000-acre Oxmoor Farm and estate in Louisville, Kentucky. As Marian's reputation grew, she began designing estates all around New England. Marian was made a junior member of the American Society of Landscape Architects in 1906, joining the two other women members, Beatrix Farrand and Elizabeth Bullard.

In 1902, Henry du Pont and his father started renovations on the Winterthur mansion and estate—2,400 acres, including 60 acres of naturalistic garden. Henry and Marian's friendship turned to business in 1910 when Henry asked Marian to help him with the landscape architecture on the property. In one correspondence, she wrote, "My dear Harry, this letter is a mixture of friendship and business, so in respect to the latter I will write you on the typewriter and save your eyesight."

The du Ponts had a long history of studying plants. "Botaniste" was the profession given on Éleuthère Irénée du Pont's passport when he came to America in 1801 and founded the du Pont empire. Louise du Pont, Henry's sister, said, "Father would take Harry and me by the hand and walk through the gardens with us, and if we couldn't identify the flowers and plants by their botanical names, we were sent to bed without our suppers."

After his father's death in 1926, Henry inherited Winterthur and started major renovations. In 1928, Marian began work on the landscape design. One major design change was the creation of a circular turnaround at the end of the driveway for the new entrance. Henry was very generous about opening his gardens for tours, and he was concerned about the traffic. He wrote to Marian questioning whether "the driveway in front of the house and also the turnabout near the tennis courts [were] big enough for those enormous buses." Marian continued to work with Winterthur until she was 79 years old, and their last project together was a redesign of the tennis court and croquet lawn.

Marian also designed the properties of other du Pont estates, Mount Cuba and Gibraltar. Her work for the du Ponts led to

Winterthur, steps to pool.
Courtesy of the Winterthur Library: Winter Archives

other commissions with some the wealthiest clients of the day, designing the estates of Senator H. Alexander Smith and Marshall Field, and the Hutton, Vanderbilt, and Carnegie estates. Marian gained national attention as the primary designer of large private estates, and in 1918, she became the second woman to be made a full fellow of the American Society of Landscape Architects. She also received an honorary doctorate degree from Hobart and William Smith Colleges. For more than 30 years, she was the landscape architect for the University of Delaware, where she was instrumental in combining the men's and women's campuses. Marian and Beatrix Farrand were the only other female college campus designers at the time.

When the Pavilion at Fort Ticonderoga in New York, "the oldest garden on this continent," was to be restored, Marian was hired to work on the project; coincidentally, Marian was a direct descendant of a commander of the fort. In 1930, Marian was honored with the Gold Medal of the Architectural League of New York. While enjoying professional accolades, Marian decided to fulfill her childhood dream of becoming a great artist. Marian took up watercolor and oil painting, and she sold her paintings through a gallery on Fifth Avenue in New York City.

In 1927, when Marian was 51 years old, she and her mother inherited money and moved to New Haven, Connecticut, to be closer to relatives. In the springtime, Marian opened her Connecticut house and garden, and hosted a party to show off her paintings and plantings. Soon, her garden parties were a well-known and much-beloved social event in New Haven.

Marian wrote about her landscaping principles in *Trees and Shrubs for Landscape Effects*. She emphasized the design of the entire property, not just isolated gardens. The chapter titles illustrate this comprehensive approach: "Gardening with Trees, Approaching the House," "The House and Its Setting," "Lawn and Terrace Treatment," "Backgrounds and Ground Covers," "Walks Formal and Informal," and "Woodland, Green and Other Gardens."

In Marian's 53-year career, she designed more than 130 landscape designs and wrote more than 70 articles. At the age of 71, Marian was asked to redesign the New York Botanical Rose Garden, which was originally designed by Beatrix Farrand in 1916. When Marian died on February 2, 1957, at age 81, she was still working on the Rose Garden. Her old and dear friend Warren H. Smith bought her house and continued hosting an annual spring garden party for 32 years in her honor.

LEARN MORE

Money, Manure, and Maintenance: Ingredients for Successful Gardens of Marian Coffin, Pioneer Landscape Architect, 1876–1957 by Nancy Fleming (Country Place Books, 1995)

The Spirit of the Garden by Martha Brooks Hutcheson (University of Massachusetts Press, 2001)

Winterthur Museum, Garden & Library, 5105 Kennett Pike, Wilmington, Delaware, www.winterthur.org

CORNELIA HAHN OBERLANDER

The Art of the Possible

One day, when Cornelia Hahn was 11 years old, she sat patiently while an artist painted her portrait. The only thing she had to look at was a maplike painting of the Rhine River on the wall. She noticed how the river curved and how the beige streets of the town met the river at right angles. The red blocks were the brick houses, and then there were green areas all over. Cornelia asked the artist, "What is the green?" The painter explained that those were the parks. Later that night, Cornelia told her mother, "When I grow up, I want to do parks."

"You want to be a landscape architect?" her mother asked.

Cornelia Hahn Oberlander.
Cornelia Hahn Oberlander Photo Library

"Yes," Cornelia replied.

"That's a difficult job," her mother explained. "And, you will have to drive a bulldozer."

"Good!" Cornelia replied, and went off to bed.

Growing up in Germany in the shadow of Adolf Hitler wouldn't keep young Cornelia away from her dream of becoming a landscape architect. She was born on June 20, 1921, in Mülheim-Ruhr, Germany, a town north of the Rhine River. Cornelia's mother was a horticulturalist, someone who studies the art and science of growing plants, and also wrote children's books on gardening. She was one of the first people to introduce the Bantam seed, a seed used to grow a sweeter corn, from America to Germany. Cornelia's father was an engineer and worked in the family steel industry, Hahnsche Werke. Her great-grandfather founded the first factory for manufacturing seamless pipes.

The branches of the Hahn family tree are filled with successful, altruistic ancestors. Cornelia's grandfather, a professor of economics and history at the University of Berlin, along with her grandmother, were involved in public housing and community work, especially in and around Berlin. Her uncle Kurt was the founder and headmaster of Salem, a prestigious boarding school in Bavaria, and her uncle Otto won the Nobel Prize in chemistry and was often called the father of nuclear chemistry.

The steel factory where Cornelia's father worked was in a dusty, industrial town, so Cornelia's mother requested that they move. They chose the village of Düsseldorf, where they had a beautiful garden full of daisies. As a small child, Cornelia spent her playtime picking flowers in the garden. Around this time, Cornelia's father moved briefly to America to study scientific management with Lillian Gilbreth. His first job was helping Lillian create her "Kitchen Practical" exhibit, which was unveiled at the Women's Exposition of 1929. Cornelia's father was very excited by what he learned there, but Cornelia's mother didn't like America and didn't want to live there. When her husband returned to Germany, the family moved to Berlin and into a house that had an even bigger garden. Cornelia had her own four-by-four-foot garden bed in which she could grow whatever she wanted. She chose to grow peas and corn.

Cornelia was homeschooled until she was eight years old. Once she started in a regular school, she was one of the few Jewish students. Some Jewish families were emigrating to other countries, seeing the rising threat of Nazism. On New Year's Eve when Cornelia was 11, her mother promised her father that they would leave Germany for America soon. Two weeks later, her father was killed in an avalanche while skiing. Cornelia was devastated, but her mother told her, "He could as easily have died crossing the street. You can't stop living."

Cornelia and her sister, Charlotte, continued with their normal activities of English and French lessons and swimming in nearby Lake Wannsee. Cornelia inherited a horse named King from some Jewish friends who had fled Germany. She taught herself how to ride and how to do circus tricks on the horse.

One Sunday afternoon when Cornelia was 14, the Nazi Gestapo pushed into the Hahn house. They were looking for evidence that they were breaking a new law that said that once per month everyone in the house must eat a one-pot soup. If they had been eating their normal roast beef dinner, they could have been arrested. The smell of the Nazis' uniforms and the black marks left from their boots created a lingering and terrifying memory for Cornelia.

On Cornelia's 16th birthday, she received a letter with a poem from her grandmother. The poem read:

With columns covered with clematis, summer houses sur-
   rounded by roses, and little rivers trickling over stones.
And you will have thought of all this out of thousands of
   remembrances. . . .
Every thing you have contact with will be woven into your
   garden. . . .
What you have created with the blood of your heart will be
   remembered by future generations.

Her grandmother's words foreshadowed Cornelia's life working and living with gardens, and formed a bittersweet good-bye
to her granddaughter, who would soon be leaving Germany.

When the *Queen Mary* docked on the New York Harbor,
17-year-old Cornelia wanted to fit right in to the American
scene, and she begged her mother to let her cut off her German
braids. They settled first in the city of New Rochelle, New York,
but Cornelia's mother felt that it was too materialistic for her
daughters. To get out of the city, her mother bought 200 acres in
New Hampshire, part of the 6,000-acre farm of the 18th-century
governor John Wentworth. Cornelia was so excited to be able
to drive something similar to a bulldozer, an old Ford tractor.
During the war, the Hahn family grew vegetables on the farm
using new organic methods.

Cornelia could think of nothing else but her dream of becoming a landscape architect. A year after arriving in the United
States, she discovered that Smith College in Massachusetts
had an interdepartmental major in architecture and landscape
architecture. Her mother suggested that Cornelia apply to some
other schools farther afield, such as the University of California, Berkeley; the University of Michigan; and Vassar College.
But Cornelia wanted to stay in New England, where she could

study with Walter Gropius and Marcel Breuer, famous architects and friends of her parents in Germany. At first she was denied admittance to Smith, allegedly because of her German accent, but when she showed them her high school grades, they let her enroll in the college.

Driving down the long road toward Smith lined with oak and London plane trees, Cornelia couldn't wait to learn all about plant materials, construction, landscape history, architectural drawing, and research. Before that, books had been her only source of study.

During field trips to design sites, the students had to carry heavy surveying tools and other equipment, in all sorts of climates. Cornelia loved studying the challenges of each site, from poor drainage to high winds, and she didn't care about the rough conditions.

Women who wanted to become landscape architects went to the Cambridge School, a part of Harvard University, because at that time women could not attend Harvard. But that changed during World War II, and in 1943, Cornelia was one of the very first women to be admitted to the Harvard Graduate School of Design. At Harvard, she studied basic design, surveying, contours, road construction, drainage, and architectural features such as steps, terraces, pools, and walls.

At Harvard, Cornelia lived with her aunt and uncle, who had also settled in America. She rode her bicycle to school, carrying her papers and drawing equipment in the front basket. Her social life centered around skiing on the weekends. On Fridays, she would leave for the Harvard ski cabin in Stowe, Vermont, at about four o'clock and return by noon on Mondays. Being in the outdoors in the forest and woods refreshed Cornelia. (Years later people have asked her where she gets her energy. Cornelia replied, "I am absolutely certain that these years of being out of doors and living on my mother's farm are the places where I gathered all the energy.")

When Cornelia was 24, while at a Harvard class picnic on Walden Pond, she met Peter Oberlander, a young Harvard student working on his master's degree in city and regional planning. Peter just had to meet the girl who brought the *gugel-hupf*—German raisin cake—and he was introduced to Cornelia. Months went by, and Peter finally called Cornelia and asked her to go see a movie with him. When he arrived for the date, Cornelia was surprised to see him carrying a T square, drawing board, and book bag. He explained, "I'm working on a management study for a new town. If you'll help me for two hours, we can still make the late show." They never made it to the movie. The couple worked on the project together for the next 48 hours, and Cornelia knew that this was the man she was destined to marry.

In 1951, Cornelia moved to Philadelphia to serve as community planner for the Citizens' Council on City Planning and worked on the Millcreek Housing Project with the famous architect Louis Kahn. One day, after a meeting, Cornelia noticed children hanging around on the street with nothing to do. She thought, "It's too bad that these kids don't have the chance to enjoy nature the way I did." She noticed the empty lot across the street; the ground was dried dirt with a few weeds. She thought, *This could be a wonderful place for mothers and children.* Cornelia went to city hall, found out who owned the empty lot, and convinced them to let her design a park for the neighborhood. That project led to her being asked to design an entire housing project, which led to many others. At 30 years old, Cornelia was finally doing what she had dreamed of since she was 11.

During this time, Peter had been working in London and Ottawa, Canada. When he was offered a teaching job at the

School of Architecture at the University of British Columbia in Vancouver, Peter asked Cornelia to marry him. On January 2, 1953, they were married at city hall, and Cornelia welcomed the adventure of moving across the continent.

In Vancouver, Cornelia began a small landscape architecture firm. She became interested in the modern art movement, which combined art and architecture to address the connections between urbanism and surrounding natural settings. Between 1956 and 1960, the Oberlanders welcomed three children: Judith, Timothy, and Wendy. While watching her children play, Cornelia realized that all children should have woods and water to play in. She thought, "If kids don't have contact with nature, how will they ever come to understand it, learn to care about it, respect it, and cooperate with it? If kids are to grow up and be caretakers rather than destroyers of the life on our beautiful blue Earth, there has to be a way to make contact with nature possible!"

> "If kids don't have contact with nature, how will they ever come to understand it, learn to care about it, respect it, and cooperate with it?"

Cornelia became a specialist in designing children's playgrounds. She was asked to design the playground at the Children's Creative Center at Expo '67 in Montreal. She wanted kids to run, climb, crawl, build, dig, and get wet. She designed sand areas, shade trees, logs to build with, and an artists' area. There was even a mound and a canal with a boat. Critics were skeptical at first, but Cornelia knew how children played. One Expo visitor was overheard saying, "A playground without swings and slides? Why, it's simply—un-Canadian!"

But soon, similar playgrounds were built around North America, after the world saw how they allowed for creative play.

A wooden boat in the canal in the Expo '67 playground designed
by Cornelia.
Cornelia Hahn Oberlander Photo Library

Also, it didn't hurt that Cornelia's imaginative designs were less
than half the cost of traditional playgrounds implemented with
their swings, slides, and jungle gyms. All totaled, she designed
more than 70 playgrounds. She also assisted in drafting national
guidelines for children's playgrounds.

During her career, Cornelia designed the landscapes of
many high-profile buildings in both Canada and the United
States. Increasingly, she practiced sustainable development,
which involves not taking more from the earth than you give
back. The rooftop gardens she designed on the Vancouver Public Library became a model for green roof designs in North
America. The public plaza Robson Square, which covers three
city blocks, has been called "a magnificent oasis in the middle

> "At its best, landscape architecture creates a dialogue between art and nature, taking inspiration from both."

of Vancouver." Cornelia fought for her plans at the National Gallery of Canada in Ottawa when the all-male board said she was crazy. Proving the worthiness of her ideas, a year after it was completed, her design won the National Award of Excellence by the Canadian Society of Landscape Architects. By concentrating on her "three Ps": patience, persistence, and politeness, Cornelia dealt with bureaucracy, which seemed to stop her every five minutes. She used research and examples to push through her innovative ideas to the masses not ready for change.

Cornelia believed that "at its best, landscape architecture creates a dialogue between art and nature, taking inspiration from both." She remains inspired by a quote from *The Brothers Karamazov* by Fyodor Dostoevsky: "Love all that has been created by God, both the whole and every grain of sand. Love every leaf and every ray of light. Love the beasts and the birds, love the plants, love every separate fragment. If you love each fragment, you will understand the mystery of the whole resting in God."

In her 60-year career, Cornelia has always practiced "the art of the possible" with patience, perseverance, and politeness, with added doses of professionalism and passion to help get her through. Cornelia continues to work and live in Vancouver, British Colombia. On October 1, 2012, she was presented with the American Society of Landscape Architects medal, that organization's highest honor.

SUSTAINABILITY IN LANDSCAPE ARCHITECTURE

Sustainable, or "green," landscaping means planning and designing outdoor spaces that are responsive to environmental concerns. These days, sustainability is a foremost concern in landscape design. Strategic site planning, tree canopy coverage, and green roofs, which are completely covered with vegetation, are some sustainable landscaping practices that create a reduction of storm water runoff, improve air and water quality, decrease the urban heat-island effect, and save energy.

The Vancouver Public Library green roof was one of 21 projects in North America nominated for a Green Roofs Award of Excellence.
Cornelia Hahn Oberlander Photo Library

Cornelia with a contractor at
the Museum of Anthropology
at the University of British
Columbia in Vancouver.
Courtesy of Elisabeth Whitelaw

LEARN MORE

Cornelia Hahn Oberlander website, www.cornelia
oberlander.ca

The Cultural Landscape Foundation Oral Histories, Cornelia Hahn Oberlander, http://tclf.org/oral-history
/cornelia-hahn-oberlander

*Love Every Leaf: The Life of Landscape Architect Cornelia Hahn
Oberlander* by Kathy Stinson (Tundra Books, 2008)

CAROL R. JOHNSON

Nature and Culture

Carol R. Johnson credits her parents with instilling in her a lifelong passion for the outdoors. Carol's father, a lawyer, and her mother, a school principal, were avid and skilled gardeners who frequently talked to her about plants and nature.

Born in a northern New Jersey suburb on September 6, 1929, Carol loved the Johnson family vacations to a farm in Vermont, where she would climb trees, hike, and camp out. The family also vacationed at a lake house on the Massachusetts island of Martha's Vineyard. Carol's memories of walking along the beach and exploring Gayhead Cliffs, where Native Americans used to live, created a nature-and-culture connection in her mind that has stayed with Carol her entire life.

Carol R. Johnson.
Carol R Johnson Associates Inc.

In her childhood, Carol exhibited a strong entrepreneurial spirit. She recalled her ambition in a 2006 interview with the Cultural Landscape Foundation, "My 11-year-old brother started a neighborhood newspaper called the *Boulevard Bugle* when he got a duplicator for Christmas one year. We lived on Midland Boulevard. His friends and I were the reporters and the delivery people. After four years, I took over. I increased the circulation from 20 to 400 and actually made money on advertising."

Carol also loved to write poems, and many of them were about large features of the landscape. One poem was about the Bayonne Bridge, which connected New Jersey and New York and opened when Carol was three. At the time, the bridge was the largest steel-construction arch bridge in the world.

Later, Carol attended Wellesley College, whose campus was designed by Frederick Law Olmsted, the leading landscape designer of the time. She was aware of the effect that the design had on the students' mentality. She studied botany in college but majored in English.

After graduating from Wellesley in 1951, Carol took off to Europe with a friend. They biked, camped, and saw wonderful things. Carol loved seeing people going about their daily activities and fitting into the urban and the rural landscapes. They saw Hampton Court in Great Britain and the Palace of Versailles in France, but Carol's experiences sleeping outdoors in sleeping bags, biking, and finding her way were just as important for her future as a landscape architect as seeing the classic buildings. She gained a true appreciation for landscapes, which may have sparked her later interest in landscape architecture.

When Carol returned from Europe, she found work at a commercial nursery in Bedford, Massachusetts. She created plant propagations (cuttings that grew new plants) and sold plants to people living in the Boston suburbs. She lived in a little shack on the property, located near the Concord-Bedford railway, which was an alleged escape route for inmates from the Concord Reformatory. Carol was often exhausted from working in the fields all day and would go to bed early. One night she was lying in bed and heard voices outside. She worried that they might have been the inmates from the nearby reformatory. Then she heard someone yell her name, and she finally came out after deciding that they were most likely not inmates. She soon learned that her visitors were students from Harvard's Graduate School of Design who were taking a summer course in plant materials. They had heard from a classmate about Carol's expansive knowledge and wanted to learn about plants from her.

"We lit a bonfire and talked over what I was doing and what they were doing and they suggested that I might study landscape architecture," Carol said when asked how she became connected with the landscape architecture program at Harvard.

Carol was admitted to Harvard's Graduate School of Design on the condition that she take a makeup math class there. Some friends had recommended that she read the book *Space, Time and Architecture* by Sigfried Giedion, and she was excited when she later discovered that the book's author would be teaching one of her classes. Carol loved studying under Giedion, and she thrived at Harvard, in part because she said Harvard was "a sort of intimate place and people looked after you and you knew everyone, and you were really part of the whole thing." At Harvard, Carol gained confidence and a keen understanding of design.

At first there were just four women in the architecture program, and Carol was the only woman student in the architectural landscape program. Her second year, however, there were so many women in the landscape program that there wasn't enough room for all of the students to work in the main studio. The administration moved the women to a smaller, out-of-the-way studio in Hunt Hall. Several women felt that this was an obviously sexist move, but Carol and many of her friends just felt lucky to be students at Harvard.

Carol graduated from the Harvard Graduate School of Design in 1957, during the postwar baby boom. A lot of schools were being built to accommodate the new children, and Carol got a job with Whitman & Howard, an engineering firm doing site planning for many schools. The next year, she worked for the Architects Collaborative (TAC). One of her projects was the landscape design for the gatehouse at Baghdad University. She stayed up all night to complete the grading of the foundation and the layout so that building could begin quickly.

Carol explained, "TAC was pretty nifty for women in those days because Norman Fletcher's wife was an architect and she was a partner. Chip Harkness's wife was an architect and she was a partner. So, there was no question that women were a part of the scene at TAC."

Given that TAC was an architecture office, its focus was not on landscape design, and Carol felt she was not being fully supported. She thought that the building was getting all the attention, while she was more concerned with the landscape. She started moonlighting as a landscape designer for family friends, working every evening and all weekend. Since her landscape design freelance work began taking up all of her time, she decided to quit working at TAC and do her own thing.

For the first five years of Carol's landscaping practice, her drafting room was in her apartment. Then she moved to a "very sweet little office" in Harvard Square, where for many years, Carol's dog went to work with her every day.

Carol recalled her first time bidding on an independent project. "I was terrorized because it was my first interview as a prime consultant for a landscape project. I worried that they

Carol (left) reviewing a plan with project team members.
Carol R. Johnson Associates Inc.

didn't give jobs like that to women, and they wouldn't give one to me," she recalled. Carol came up with a strategy: she brought her two male employees with her so that the client would take her seriously. Still, the male-owned firm won the job. A woman on the deciding board later told Carol that they gave the job to "two good men rather than one good woman." And Carol thought that it was the men that she had to prove herself to!

Still, Carol wasn't deterred from her dream career. Her practice started to take off after she completed a project for a church, then a swimming pool, followed by gardens for some fast-growing subdivisions. Then, Carol hit the big time when the architecture firm Cambridge Seven Associates asked her to design the landscape for the new Buckminster Fuller dome at the American Pavilion for Expo '67 in Montreal. Carol flew around the Canadian countryside, selecting trees from farmers for her design.

Many of Carol's early projects involved the energy industry and the environment. For the Chevron Oil Refinery in Perth Amboy, New Jersey, she designed plantings and buffers, and also came up with a color palette that camouflaged the facility into its environment. She invented a color called dawn grey, which was used on the entire refinery to blend the structures perfectly with the skies. Still, growing her fledgling business wasn't easy. She said, "I had a hard time getting even part-time employees. I was an unknown woman, and there were plenty of jobs with famous men."

During those early days, Carol flew frequently to Washington, DC, for meetings and she was usually the only woman on

A detailed view of the quadrangle entrance at Agnes Scott College, designed by Carol Johnson.
Carol R. Johnson Associates Inc.

FLORENCE YOCH

In 1915, Florence Yoch graduated from the University of Illinois at Urbana-Champaign with a landscape architecture degree. After returning to her home state of California, she began practicing landscape design in 1918, and she completed more than 250 projects in 53 years. Her projects included grand estates for Hollywood figures including producers Jack Warner and David O. Selznick and director George Cukor, college campuses, parks, and even a botanical garden. Florence also created the landscape designs for the classic movie *Gone with the Wind*, built on a studio set in Los Angeles with a budget of $16,000 (the equivalent of over $260,000 in 2013).

those flights. Now when she flies down there, she says, the plane is filled with businesswomen.

Carol R. Johnson Associates Inc. has worked on a wide range of projects including college campuses, cemeteries, gyms, commercial and corporate landscapes, historic preservation, parks, and land restoration. Carol explained in her oral history, "My own work has been said to possess simplicity, elegance, quiet surprises, and clarity."

Additionally, Carol has gained a reputation for designing landscapes that accommodate people with disabilities. She has a unique philosophy: "I want to make the accessible route so interesting and appealing that the 'able bodied' will find some value in using it as well. I don't like to have something pushed off to the side, sort of in the backyard for the accessible route."

Carol became a fellow of the American Society of Landscape Architects (ASLA) in 1982, and in 1998 she was the first American

> "You can learn so much when you are a landscape architect. There's a diversity of focus and opportunities for artistic expression in three dimensions."

woman to receive the ASLA Gold Medal. Her firm celebrated its 50th anniversary in 2009 and has become one of the largest landscape architectural firms in the United States, with clients around the world. In her oral history, Carol wanted to start by explaining what she loves about landscape architecture: "You can learn so much when you are a landscape architect. There's a diversity of focus and opportunities for artistic expression in three dimensions."

In a 2010 interview for *Landscape Architecture* magazine, she explained her thoughts on the current state of landscape architecture. She said, "I am surprised at the increasing interest in landscape architecture among the types of people I run into—it has become a much more visible profession than it used to be."

In 1993, Carol turned management of her firm over to her partners for them to lead the company in further growth. Carol

CAROL R. JOHNSON: MENTOR

Engineer Judy Nitsch threw an 80th birthday party for Carol in 2008. Many leaders of women-owned companies were invited. When asked about their relationship, Carol said, "I always knew who she was although I hadn't met her. After I started my business, I decided to call her and see if she'd meet with me—she did! She was generous with her advice, and to this day we refer to and adhere to her advice on certain things."

R. Johnson Associates Inc. now has offices in Boston; Knoxville, Tennessee; and Abu Dhabi, United Arab Emirates. Now in her 80s, Carol still works where and when the client has asked for her specifically to design the project. Now that she finally has time to take vacations, Carol enjoys traveling to places like Kenya, Grenada, Rome, Florence, Nepal, Vietnam, France, and Moscow.

LEARN MORE

Landscape Legends: Carol Johnson Oral History Interview. The Cultural Landscape Foundation, 2006, http://tclf.org/sites/default/files/pioneers/johnson _carol/videos/index.html

Principles of Ecological Landscape Design by Travis Beck (Island Press, 2013)

"Shared Wisdom" by Jane Roy Brown, Interview with Carol R. Johnson, *Landscape Architecture*, December 2010

MARTHA SCHWARTZ

Modern Art and Landscape

M artha Schwartz always wanted to be an artist. As a child, she took art classes on Saturday mornings in the basement of the Philadelphia Museum of Art, and afterward she would roam the halls. Her favorite place to visit in the museum was the Japanese teahouse and garden, which felt almost magical. Set deep within the museum in a softly lit room, the teahouse had a calm, trancelike effect on the young girl. She also loved wandering the greenhouses at Longwood Gardens on the du Pont Estate in Kennett Square, Pennsylvania. She imagined living in a house made out of nature. Her bed would be set atop a huge carpet of grass so that she could wake up and step upon fresh grass when she awoke.

Martha Schwartz.
Courtesy of Martha Schwartz Partners

One of six daughters, born in Philadelphia, Pennsylvania, on November 21, 1950, Martha comes from a family filled with creative people. Her great-grandfathers came from Russia and Romania in the beginning of the 20th century and expressed their artistry through their work as tailors. Many family members are architects, including her father, sister, uncle, cousin, and son, as well as her husband and many close friends. Other branches of the family tree are filled with graphic designers, painters, engineers, and even a few psychologists.

Martha's father ran an architectural office in Philadelphia designing high-rise housing projects. On the floor of his office, Martha would play with old, dried-out Magic Markers and broken toilet templates—standard architecture tools to help draftsmen outline toilets on floor plans. Surrounded by boring catalogs of doorjambs and window jambs and strict project time lines, Martha knew that it was not the environment that she wanted to work in when she grew up.

Growing up, Martha mainly went to Quaker schools in addition to those art classes she took at the Philadelphia College of Art during high school. After graduating from high school, Martha majored in printmaking at the School of Architecture and Design at the University of Michigan. She became intrigued by artists who were outside the New York gallery scene and creating large, landscape-inspired sculptures. Artists such as Walter De Maria, Michael Heizer, Mary Miss, and Richard Long were creating art in their natural environments and introducing a new environmental awareness to viewers. Martha especially loved Robert Smithson's *Spiral Jetty*, which was built entirely out of natural materials (mud, water, rocks, and salt crystals) found on the northeastern short of the Great Salt Lake in Utah. She was drawn to how the landscape-inspired sculpture worked with the environment to simultaneously make a piece of art, while drawing attention to the land itself.

After five years in the fine arts department at the University of Michigan, Martha decided to enroll in the university's three-year landscape architecture graduate program so she could focus on environmental art. But Martha soon discovered that most students were in the landscape program to *save* the environment, and only one other student was an art student. When she asked to take extra art classes, her request was denied. The chairman of the school at that time did not think that art had anything to do with landscape architecture.

In 1973, Martha worked as a summer intern at the landscape planning and design firm SWA Group. The firm was located in Sausalito, near San Francisco, and was founded by Peter Walker, one of the leaders of the landscape architecture movement. Martha recalled how, at the first meeting with all the interns, Peter berated them for doing what was expected rather than bringing anything of interest or value to the world. When the students were invited to dinner at Peter's house, Martha was shocked to see a painting by abstract artist Frank Stella on the wall. Martha reflected later, "I was completely dumbfounded that a landscape architect

> "I was completely dumbfounded that a landscape architect would know anything about contemporary art."

would know anything about contemporary art—and minimalism to boot. He was the first landscape architect I had met who made any connection to the art world. And, given his stature in the profession, his opinion that art was somehow related to landscape architecture greatly reassured me that perhaps I might find a home within the profession."

In the winter of 1978, after transferring to the Harvard Graduate School of Design, where Peter was teaching, Martha experienced another pivotal moment. Peter took the class to Vermont to visit modernist landscape architect Dan Kiley. Dan showed the class slides of the work of André Le Nôtre, the 17th-century French gardener of King Louis XIV. Le Nôtre designed the very formal gardens at the Palace of Versailles, among many others. Martha explained her reaction: "I was so knocked out by these images that I could hardly control myself. I had just seen a landscape that was intentional, did not look like nature, was minimal to an extreme, and was so huge that it ate everything around it. It was more beautiful than the Grand Canyon. It all came together in that moment."

While Martha experienced a transformation in relation to her artwork, so too did her relationship change with her beloved teacher: Peter Walker and Martha were married in 1979. By then, Martha felt strongly that she wanted to express her artistic side in her work. Thinking and scheming about the design of her own front yard was making her happy. She had never created an art installation (an artwork displayed in a large space), and she knew that it had to be done with very little money since she was paying for it herself. Afraid that Peter would turn down her idea of designing an installation for their front yard, Martha decided to keep it a secret. She set up her work materials in the attic of their home, which Peter rarely entered, and when he left for a trip, Martha quickly set to work. In the center of the front-yard garden, she planted a grid of bright pink geraniums surrounded by boxwood hedges. Then, Martha placed eight dozen bagels, which she had secretly dipped in varnish in their attic, in a double row on the ground between the rows of hedges. When Peter arrived home that evening, he was greeted by Martha and their friends who where there for a party in their new Bagel Garden.

During the party, Martha asked a friend if he would mind taking pictures of the project. She was later encouraged to send the photos to *Landscape Architecture* magazine. Though Martha didn't expect a response from the magazine, the editor replied that he wanted to publish a photo of the Bagel Garden and asked if Martha would write an article about the design. In a less than serious tone, Martha wrote about how the bagel was an appropriate landscape material because it was cheap and easy to install, was a democratic material, did well in the shade, and didn't need watering.

When the article was published it created quite a stir in the landscape community. In a bold move by the editor, the photo was highlighted on the front cover. Many magazine subscribers, who felt that the Bagel Garden was below the dignity of the profession, cancelled their memberships. Though the editor of the magazine was fired, the publication of the Bagel Garden article made Martha an instant star. The following month, the magazine's editorial section overflowed with a heated debate about the garden. Some designers, who were working hard to take the profession to new levels, felt that the work set the field of landscape architecture back 20 years. Others felt that the garden was a breath of fresh air in a design community that was becoming stale.

The publication of the Bagel Garden article marked the first time a landscape design project earned star status based not on the garden design but on the garden as an art image. This changed the face of landscape architecture from something more traditional to an exciting, energetic, and growing field. Critics point out that just because a project gets a lot of press and exposure that does not mean that it is good design. Other fields like architecture and fashion don't have a problem with showing off their designs.

From then on, Martha continued making unique statements combining contemporary art and landscapes. In a daylong installation in Cambridge, Massachusetts, to celebrate May Day 1980, Martha arranged Necco Wafers candy in a geometric pattern using a 17th-century French formal garden theme. An Ultimate Frisbee tournament took place in the garden later in the day, after installation was complete.

"I've always wanted to make the point that it's possible to have children, to be a woman, and to kick butt at work."

In Martha's design for Atlanta's Rio Shopping Center, she used more than 350 golden frogs. Her "landscapes" typically comprise sidewalks, roads, shopping malls, byways, highways,

Marina Linear Park, San Diego, California, 1988.
Courtesy of Martha Schwartz Partners

and parking lots—the areas that surround the buildings in cities—rather than the traditional definition of landscape: forests, oceans, rivers, sand dunes, prairies, and natural spaces.

In the 1990s, Martha and Peter had two sons, Jake and Joseph. With that addition, Martha's studios had to function as living space too. She explained, "It's the only way I knew how to combine work and family. I've always wanted to make the point that it's possible to have children, to be a woman, and to kick butt at work."

When Martha and Peter divorced in 2000, Martha kept primary custody of the kids, and her sons essentially grew up in her office. These days, Jake has his own successful architectural practice in Beijing, and Joseph is an actor. Now remarried, Martha is raising a daughter in the studio home with her new husband, Markus Jatsch.

In 2005, Martha designed the Grand Canal Square in Dublin, one of the largest paved public spaces in the city. It has been called the most innovative landscape design to be built in Dublin. The central pathway of the plaza is lined with 25-foot-tall

WOMEN IN THE DIRT

Today, women are influencing the profession of landscape architecture more than ever before. *Women in the Dirt* is a 2012 documentary focusing on the work of seven contemporary, award-winning designers who have made their mark in the field: Mia Lerher, Andrea Cochran, Cheryl Barton, Isabelle Greene, Katherine Spitz, Pamela Palmer, and Lauren Melendrez. Each woman has made great contributions to the field, while sharing a passion for sustainability and enduring design.

Grand Canal Square,
Dublin, Ireland, 2005.
Courtesy of Martha Schwartz Partners

red, glowing, angled light sticks made of a newly developed red resin-glass material. When asked to explain the space, Martha says, "The use of light and space lures the public to Grand Canal Square, creating an interactive space that functions as a social magnet during the day and night. . . . In addition, the fact that it opens onto a large, nontidal body of water makes it a unique space for Ireland."

Initially labeled *l'enfant terrible* (the terrible child) of landscape architecture for her Bagel Garden, Martha is now considered the "mother of innovation." Calling on the influence of important pop artists such as Andy Warhol and Jasper Johns, she uses bright colors and manmade materials to mix pop-art elements with modernism and cubism into her work. She also credits her "pretty funny family" as a source for the humor in her work. Martha's many awards include the Cooper-Hewitt National Design Award and the Women in Design Award for Excellence from the Boston Society of Architects.

With more than 30 years of experience as a landscape architect and artist, Martha is currently principal at Martha Schwartz

Partners, which has offices in the United States, United Kingdom, and China. Her projects span 20 countries and four continents.

Of her work, Martha says, "Although my interests have broadened and deepened over time, I am still guided by the desire to make cities that speak to people, draw them in and make them feel. My focus is primarily on cities because that's where the greatest populations live—by 2050, 78 percent of the world's population will be living in cities. To make cities appealing, and therefore sustainable, they have to be places where people can work, relax, and enjoy a beautiful surrounding."

LEARN MORE

Of Gardens by Paula Deitz (University of Pennsylvania Press, 2011)

Recycling Spaces: Curating Urban Evolution: The Work of Martha Schwartz Partners by Emily Waugh and Martha Schwartz (ORO Editions, 2012)

The Vanguard Landscapes and Gardens of Martha Schwartz edited by Tim Richardson (Thanes & Hudson, 2004)

Women in the Dirt: Landscape Architects Shaping Our World directed by Carolann Stoney (Wind Media Productions, 2011)

ACKNOWLEDGMENTS

CONFUCIUS SAID, "Choose a job you love, and you will never have to work a day in your life." I have to thank everyone who every day made this project a labor of love.

A huge thank-you to Lisa Reardon, my extremely patient editor at Chicago Review Press, who was a wonderful cheerleader for this project, and Amelia Estrich, my project editor, who helped me polish it into shape.

Thank you to all the librarians and research librarians at the St. Charles Public Library. The interlibrary loan is such an amazing resource available to the public.

I am grateful and honored that I was able to talk to some of "my women." Their excitement over the project was intoxicating. Thank you, Judy Nitsch, Aine Brazil, Cornelia Hahn Oberlander, Carol R. Johnson, Denise Scott Brown, Marilyn Jordan Taylor, and the late Natalie de Blois.

Thank you to the families of "my women" for your generous help with finding images and helping with research. Nancy Perkins, Anna Keichline's grandniece; Marcia and Madeline Schnapp, Ruth Gordon Schnapp's daughters; Dr. Cornelius Welch and David Fairweather, Norma Sklarek's husband and son; Jan Gleason, wife of James S. Gleason, the grand-nephew of Kate Gleason; Ellen S. Rhodes, Ellen Shipman's great-granddaughter; Jim Venturi, Denise Scott Brown's son; and Markus Jatsch, Martha Schwartz's husband.

Thank you to the amazing people who helped me through the image process: Hoyt Fields (Hearst Castle), David Bagnall (Frank Lloyd Wright Preservation Trust), Judith B. Tankard (Beatrix Farrand Society), Jason Flahardy (University of Kentucky Archives), Elizabeth Wolf (Mary and Leigh Block Museum of Art), Dale Ann Stieber and Annie Mar (Occidental College Library), Ellen Sandberg (the Granger Collection), Heather A. Clewell and Jeanne Solensky (Winterthur), James Kent, Alexander Konidaris and Bess Adler (Thornton Tomasetti), Molly Cort and Marnie Soom (RIT Cary Graphic Arts Press), Neal Harmeyer (Purdue University Libraries), David Kuzma (Special Collections and University Archives, Rutgers University Libraries) Manon Janssens and Claudia Fruianu (Zaha Hadid Architects), Kait Ellis (executive assistant to Dean Marilyn Jordan Taylor), Elizabeth Kubany and Jessica Pleasants (Skidmore, Owings & Merrill), and a few I'm sure I forgot.

Betty Shanahan at the Society of Women Engineers; Martha Thorne, the executive director at Pritzker Architecture Prize; Nancy Hadley at the American Institute of Architects—thank you for your suggestions as I was selecting subjects among so many fascinating women.

Thank you and hugs to everyone who cheered me on at the Internet water cooler, and, most importantly, my dear friends who lent an ear and a heart along the way.

Finally, a huge thank-you to my computer-savvy husband, Robert, and my creative kids, Emily, Hayden, and Everett, for your patience and for filling my life with creativity and fun.

And, an extra thank-you to Emily for letting me borrow her lucky number 22 and to Lucy, who waited patiently at my feet with her ball, so I could write.

RESOURCES

PROGRAMS FOR KIDS AND TEENS

ArchKIDecture
ArchKIDecture encourages and explains math, science, and visual-arts concepts through the medium of architecture. The site includes fun online projects, lesson plans, recommended books, and more.
www.archkidecture.org

Archikids
Archikids is a New York City–based program of fun and creative programs with an emphasis on 3-D visualization and building for kids of all ages.
www.archikids.org

Chicago Architecture Foundation (CAF)
CAF provides many engaging programs for educators, families, groups, and kids to explore Chicago's architecture.
www.architecture.org

CAF Teens
The teen chapter of CAF includes studio programs, competitions, and experiences to engage teens about the fields of architecture, engineering, and construction.
www.architecture.org/cafteens

eGFI (Engineering, Go For It!)
This program was started by the American Society for Engineering Education (ASEE) to promote and enhance efforts to improve K-12 STEM (Science, Technology, Engineering, and Math) and engineering education. Includes engineering news, a student-written blog, and newsletter.
www.egfi-k12.org

Engineering Girl
Geared toward teenage girls, this is an online resource for links, profiles of women engineers, and interactive features introducing the basics of an engineering career.
www.engineergirl.org

Engineer Your Life
This is an online source of videos of inspiring women engineers, descriptions of dream engineering jobs, and many other resources for high school girls considering a career in engineering.
www.engineeryourlife.org

Imagine Engineering
A website and workshops run by the Girl Scouts organization providing mentors, advice about pursuing an engineering career, and other resources.
www.girlscouts.org/imagineengineering

Introduce a Girl to Engineering Day
During National Engineering Week (in February), one day is devoted to engaging and mentoring girls through workshops, lab tours, online discussions, and interactive, hands-on activities at businesses, universities, libraries, and other venues across the country.
www.eweek.org/EngineersWeek/IntroduceAGirl.aspx

Salvadori Center, New York City
The Salvadori Center helps teachers and kids explore math and science concepts, architecture, and engineering through investigation of buildings, bridges, and skyscrapers. It offers in- and out-of-school programs for New York City–area students, but there are cool things anyone can do online as well, such as exploring the Brooklyn Bridge.
www.salvadori.org/kids

Try Engineering
An online resource for students, parents, teachers, and school counselors interested in engineering careers.
www.tryengineering.org

PLACES TO VISIT IN PERSON OR ONLINE

Beatrix Farrand Society
Bar Harbor, Maine
Beatrix's last home, Garland Farm, became the Beatrix Farrand Society in 2003—a nonprofit organization created to foster the art and science of horticulture and landscape design. Tours and programs are open to the public.
www.beatrixfarrandsociety.org

Contemporary Arts Center
Cincinnati, Ohio
The first museum designed by a woman in the United States and Zaha Hadid's first design in the United States.
www.contemporaryartscenter.org

Frank Lloyd Wright Home and Studio
Oak Park, Illinois
Private tours of and educational programs are available at Frank Lloyd Wright's private residence and workplace for the first 20 years of his architectural career. Several Wright-designed homes line the neighboring streets in Oak Park.
http://gowright.org/home-and-studio.html

Hearst Castle
San Simeon, California
Part of the California State Parks System, Hearst Castle is open to the public 362 days a year. Several tour types are available, including curriculum-based school tours.
www.hearstcastle.org

National Building Museum
Washington, DC
This family-friendly museum near the National Mall in DC is devoted to the history and impact of the built environment. Exhibits, public programs, and festivals are dedicated to the stories of architecture, engineering, and design.
www.nbm.org

Roebling Museum
Roebling, New Jersey
Formerly the gateway to the Roebling Steel Mill, the Roebling museum houses exhibits and collections about the family business. Tours, lectures, and programs are designed for elementary and high school students.
www.roeblingmuseum.org

Winterthur Museum, Garden, and Library
Winterthur, Delaware
Tours of and programs about the Du Pont Family Estate and Gardens, are offered for elementary to high school students. The 60-acre naturalistic garden is one of the most renowned in the country.
www.winterthur.org

PROFESSIONAL ORGANIZATIONS

Association for Women in Architecture, Los Angeles
The Association for Women in Architecture is a nonprofit organization dedicated to advancing and supporting positions of women in the architecture and design fields.
http://awa-la.org

Beverly Willis Architecture Foundation
This nonprofit foundation was created to advance the position of women in architecture.
www.bwaf.org

Chicago Women in Architecture
Founded 30 years ago, Chicago Women in Architecture is a nonprofit organization for women in architecture and related professions.
www.cwarch.org

IEEE Women in Engineering (WIE)
The IEEE is the largest international professional organization dedicated to promoting women engineers and scientists and inspiring girls around the world to follow their academic interests to a career in engineering.
www.ieee.org/women

National Association of Women in Construction (NAWIC)
Founded by 16 women in 1953, the National Association of Women in Construction is an international association that promotes and supports the advancement and employment of women in the construction industry.
www.nawic.org

Organization of Women Architects and Design Professionals
For more than 40 years, the Organization of Women Architects and Design Professionals has been an active support network in the San Francisco Bay Area for the many women involved in architecture, building engineering, planning, landscape architecture, interior and graphic design, and related environmental design fields.
http://owa-usa.org

Society of Women Engineers (SWE)
The Society of Women Engineers is a nonprofit educational and service organization that works to help women succeed and advance in engineering careers.
http://societyofwomenengineers.swe.org

Women in Architecture (a committee of the AIA)
A committee of the New York chapter of the American Institute of Architects.
http://wianyc.wordpress.com

Women in Architecture (at the University of Illinois)
Founded in 1998 by architecture students at the University of Illinois at Urbana-Champaign, the WIA provides events and networking opportunities for students at all levels, as well as professors.
www2.arch.uiuc.edu/organizations/wia

Women in Landscape Architecture (WILA)
Women in Landscape Architecture's Professional Practice Network creates resources for women in the profession, provides mentorship opportunities, encourages discussion of work-life balance concerns, and establishes a virtual home for its members.
www.asla.org/women

NOTES

INTRODUCTION

In the construction: M. W. Howard, *Transactions of the New-York State Agricultural Society, with an Abstract of the Proceedings, of the County Agricultural Societies,* vol. 7, 1847 (C. Van Benthuysen, 1848), 228.

I was fired with the desire: Brookes Hutcheson and Clarence Fowler, "Three Women in Landscape Architecture," *Alumnae Bulletin of the Cambridge School of Domestic and Landscape Architecture* 4, no. 2 (April 1932).

It must be obvious: "Occupations of Women: What the Field of Architecture Offers to the Well Trained, Practical Woman," *New-York Daily Tribune,* August 26, 1901, 7.

a gardener: Mrs. Schuyler Van Rensselaer, *Art Out-of-Doors: Hints on Good Taste in Gardening* (New York: Charles Scribner's Sons, 1893), 18.

the arts of architecture: Jones Farrand, "The Garden in Relation to the House," *Garden and Forest,* January 15, 1897, 132–133.

ARCHITECTS

As a means: Lois L. Howe, "The Architect," in Catherine Filene, ed., *Careers for Women* (Boston: Houghton Mifflin Co., 1920), 47.

Louise Bethune

A caustic remark: Frances E. Willard and Mary A. R. Livermore. *A Woman of the Century: Fourteen Hundred-Seventy Biographical Sketches Accompanied by Portraits of Leading American Women in All Walks of Life* (Buffalo, NY: Charles Wells Moulton, 1893), 80–81.

Mrs. Bethune refuses: Ibid.

It was a quarter to four: "Ladies of the Wheel," *Buffalo Illustrated Express*, August 14, 1892.

In order to have any: Louise Bethune, "Women and Architecture," *Inland Architect and News Record 17* (March 1891), 20.

There is no need: Ibid.

The total number of: Ibid.

Anna Wagner Keichline

Such a liking: "May Devote Life to Industrial Arts," *Philadelphia Inquirer,* October 19, 1903.

At college we worked: Keichline, Eleanor Morton, "More About the Advantages of Having a Woman as Architect for the Home," n.d.

With reference to Letter to the Military Intelligence Division of the U.S. Army, Miss Anna Wagner Keichline to Captain Harry A. Taylor, February 4, 1918. Provided by Nancy Jane Perkins, great-niece of Anna Keichline.

Add to the roster: "Architects and Avocations," *American Architect and Architecture* (December 1936), 52.

The equipment of: Keichline, Eleanor Morton, "More About the Advantages of Having a Woman as Architect for the Home," n.d.

Julia Morgan

Every architect: Morgan North to Suzanne B. Reiss, *Julia Morgan architectural history project interviews* : [electronic resource] oral history transcript / tape recorded interview conducted 1974–75, 168.

homesickness and nervous: Julia Morgan to Phoebe Hearst. Sara
Holmes Boutelle, *Julia Morgan Architect* (New York: Abbeville,
1988), 170–171. The original letter is in the archives of the Bancroft
Library, University of California, Berkeley.

get up, tremble: Ibid., 31.

to whom I have to pay: *Julia Morgan: Life by Design*, PBS documentary,
1990.

Miss Morgan, we are tired: Hearst to Morgan, Patricia Failing, "She
Was American's Most Successful Woman Architect—And Hardly
Anyone Knows Her Name," *Artnews 80*, January 1981, 70.

I wanted to work: Manley, Molly Sinclair, "Miami: An Unplanned
Disaster?" *Miami Herald*, January 28, 1973, E24.

Never turn down a job: Morgan, Walter T. Steilberg, "Some Examples
of the Work of Julie Morgan," *Architect and Engineer*, November 1918.

Marion Mahony Griffin

She was the most: H. Allen Brooks, *The Prairie School: Frank Lloyd
Wright and His Midwest Contemporaries* (Toronto: University of
Toronto Press, 1972), 3.

In the loveliest spot: Marion Mahony Griffin, *The Magic of America:
Electronic Edition*. August 2007. IV. 281–282. The Art Institute of
Chicago and the New York Historical Society, 29 October 2008.

When the five: Mahony Griffin, *The Magic of America*, IV. 137.

rebelled and told: Mahony Griffin, James Weirick, "Marion Mahoney
at MIT," *Transition* 25:4 (1988).

Five men, two women: Wright, John Lloyd, *My Father, Frank Lloyd
Wright* (New York: Dover Publications, 1992), 35.

She was so ugly: Letter from John Lloyd Wright to Mark Peisch, January 22, 1969, Avery Architectural Library, Columbia University,
New York.

Back to the office: Mahony Griffin, *The Magic of America: Electronic
Edition*. August 2007. IV. 281–282. The Art Institute of Chicago and
the New York Historical Society, 29 October 2008.

When I encountered: Mahony Griffin, *The Magic of America*, IV.157.

For the love of Mike: Ibid, 294.

Women should continue: Ibid, 157.

Norma Merrick Sklarek

It's a sexist title: Norma Merrick Sklarek Oral History, National Visionary Leadership Project.

Although both my parents: Sklarek, Dorothy Ehrhart-Morrison, *No Mountain High Enough* (Conari Press, 1997), 30.

What about: Ibid.

Other colleges at: Ibid, 91.

Denise Scott Brown

There were all: Scott Brown, *Oral History Interview with Denise Scott Brown*, 1990 Oct. 25–1991 Nov. 9, Archives of American Art, Smithsonian Institution.

If I had any pangs: Scott Brown, *Oral History Interview with Denise Scott Brown*.

I told them that: Scott Brown, Meg Frankowski, "Philadelphia Architect Robert Venturi Retires at Age 87," *NewsWorks*, July 26, 2012.

Well, then: Scott Brown, *Oral History Interview with Denise Scott Brown*.

When asked: Scott Brown, Interview by Adam Marcus, Denise Scott Brown and Robert Venturi, *Museo Magazine* 14, Spring 2010.

First, I fell in love: Robert Venturi, Interview, Denise Scott Brown and Robert Venturi.

I believe our creative: Tyng, Louis I. Kahn, *Louis Kahn to Anne Tyng: The Rome Letters, 1953–1954*, Rizzoli, 55.

It's like producing a jungle gym: Scott Brown, "Philadelphia Architect Robert Venturi Retires at Age 87."

The social trivia: Scott Brown, "Room at the Top? Sexism and the Star System in Architecture," in *Architecture: A Place for Women*, ed. Ellen Perry Berkeley, 1989.

I have been helped: Ibid.

those things and a few more: Scott Brown, *Oral History Interview with Denise Scott Brown*.

Natalie de Blois

Long, lean, quizzical: Nathaniel Owings, *The Spaces in Between* (Boston: Houghton Mifflin, 1973), 264–265.

My father, being an engineer: de Blois, Interviewed by Betty J. Blum, *The Oral History of Natalie de Blois* (Art Institute of Chicago, 2004).

One of the first times: de Blois, ibid.

I liked it: de Blois, Interview with Detlef Mertins in *Skidmore, Owings & Merrill Journal* 4, 2004.

After working my: de Blois, *Oral History,* ibid.

The first publicity: de Blois, ibid.

And that was: de Blois, Interview with Detlef Mertins, ibid.

I see architecture: Jeanne, Michael Arndt, "Name to Know: Architect Jeanne Gang," *Bloomberg BusinessWeek: Innovation,* November 3, 2009.

It wasn't tough: de Blois, Interview with Staffan Schmidt, *Modernity Retired: Chicago Five,* Professional Dreamers, January 6, 2010.

He didn't seem: Ibid.

How do I bring: Ibid.

Zaha Hadid

the Muslim and Jewish: Hadid, "Design's Hip Diva Hits America's Heartland: This Month in Cincinnati, Radical Architect Zaha Hadid Demonstrates the Fine Art of Breaking the Rules," *Newsweek,* May 19, 2003.

My father took: Hadid, "Zaha Hadid on the Trials of Being a Woman Architect," *Guardian* (London), October 8, 2006.

I was very young: Hadid, "Iraqitect: Zaha Hadid Commands the Guggenheim, but Remembers Her Roots," *Sunday Times Magazine* (London), June 4, 2006.

It was such: Hadid, "Towering Ambition," *Evening Standard* (London), August 25, 2006.

If it doesn't kill you: Hadid, *Guardian.*

I can be: Hadid, Ibid.

For an architect: Hadid, Ibid.

I'm trying to discover: Hadid, Ibid.

Marilyn Jordan Taylor

When I saw: Jordan Taylor, "New Design Dean," *University of Pennsylvania Gazette,* June 27, 2008.

Deborah Berke is: Jordan Taylor, "Deborah Berke Awarded New Berkeley-Rupp Prize," *ArchDaily*, September 12, 2012.

I loved working: Jordan Taylor, "Thinking Big," *Penn Current*, University of Pennsylvania, March 26, 2009.

I'm incredibly proud: Ibid.

I'm not really: Jordan Taylor, Marilyn Jordan Taylor, Skidmore, Owings & Merrill, "Most Powerful Women in New York 2007," *Crain's New York Business*, September 16, 2007.

ENGINEERS

Emily Warren Roebling

As soon as Mrs. Roebling: *New York Times*, July 3, 1883.

the Eighth Wonder of the World: "The Bridge: Some Interesting Facts about the Enterprise," *Brooklyn Daily Eagle*, August 11, 1876, 4.

It is thus: Hewitt, Abram S., "Address on the Opening of the New York and Brooklyn Bridge, May 24, 1883" (New York: J. Polhemus, 1883), 56–58.

I never heard her: Emily Warren Roebling to John A. Roebling II, April 9, 1899. Special Collections and Archives, Rutgers University Library.

Lillian Moller Gilbreth

shy child: Gilbreth, *As I Remember* (Norcross, GA: Engineering and Manufacturing Press, 1998), 19–21.

never lonely: Ibid., 23.

comic . . . bluestocking: Ibid., 41.

if she couldn't: Ibid., 26.

This is disturbing: Ibid., 56.

a burden of fear: Ibid., 19–21.

Unfortunately, the graduation night: Ibid., 58.

Mama was sympathetic: Ibid., 66.

The experience was: Ibid., 68.

he needed it more: Ibid., 72.

I want to teach you: Frank Gilbreth, Edna Yost, *Frank and Lillian Gilbreth: Partners for Life* (Rutgers University Press, 1949), 114.

Frank, always planning: Frank Gilbreth, *As I Remember,* 107.

Did you get it?: Ibid., 139.

His matrimonial catastrophe: "Warns Wives of Careers," *New York Times,* July 28, 1911.

Kate Gleason

Girls were not: Gleason, Eve Chappell, "Kate Gleason Careers," *Woman Citizen,* January 1926, 20.

Oh, if Kate had: Gleason, Helen Christine Bennett, "Kate Gleason's Adventures in a Man's Job," *American Magazine,* October 1928, 168.

I'm awfully sorry: Ibid., 169.

Any advertising is good: Ibid., 170.

Marriage is a career: Gleason, "Kate Gleason's Adventures," 37.

When I recall stories: Ibid.

Margaret Ingels

Margaret Ingels: Alice C. Goff, *Women Can Be Engineers,* 1946.

Associates who have: "Personalities in Industry: Margaret Ingels, M.E.," *Scientific American,* April 1941, 197.

It was no: Ibid.

flair for construction work: *Kentucky Kernel,* September 30, 1927, 2.

"Maggie" has the distinction: *Kentuckian,* vol. 12, Senior Class, 1916, 65.

No, I'm not: Ingels, *Kentucky Kernel,* April 13, 1916, 8.

We are pleased: *Kentucky Kernel,* Sept. 30, 1927, 2.

The woman who: Ingels, "Petticoats and Slide Rules," Margaret E. Layne, P.E., ed., *Women in Engineering: Pioneers and Trailblazers,* (American Society of Civil Engineers, 2009).

Ruth Gordon Schnapp

Every branch of engineering: Ruth Gordon Schnapp, Interview with Deborah Rice, Society of Women Engineers, 2006.

In college, I: Schnapp, Interview with Deborah Rice, Society of Women Engineers, 2006.

My parents said that: Schnapp, guest speaker, Los Banos Rotary Club August 14, 2009.

At that time: Schnapp interview, 2006.

When I wrote to Stanford: Ibid.

You laid on: Ibid.

Well, we're: Ibid.

Well . . . women: Ibid.

One of my friends: Schnapp, guest speaker, 2009.

I was in charge: Ibid.

I don't think I passed: Schnapp interview, 2006.

I really loved: Ibid.

I've made it! I've made it!: Ibid.

It's a very rewarding: Ibid.

I became very: Schnapp, guest speaker, 2009.

Judith Nitsch

I can remember: Nitsch, telephone interview, October 15, 2012.

My sister was: Ibid.

My sister would: Ibid.

She totally encouraged it: Ibid.

Mr. Perry didn't: Ibid.

You figure out: Nitsch's mother, Dot Nitsch, to Nitsch, ibid.

I started out: Nitsch, ibid.

I thought mechanical: Ibid.

They had about: Nitsch, "Judith Nitsch," *Profiles of Civil Engineers*, Sloan Career Cornerstone Center, American Society of Civil Engineers.

They wondered if: Nitsch interview with Joan Killough-Miller, "Paving the Way," *Transformations*, Worchester Polytechnic Institute, Spring 2008.

As I explained why: Nitsch, phone interview 2012.

Tony was the: Ibid.

I would always drag: Ibid.

We didn't want: Nitsch, Mary K. Pratt, "These Women Make Mark Despite Persistent Notions," *Boston Business Journal*, September 7, 2009.

About one-third: Nitsch, "Paving the Way."

I will speak: Ibid.

Remember: Ibid.

Oh, I love what I do: Ibid.

Aine Brazil

I think I've always: "Galway's Aine Brazil Leaves Her Mark on City's Skyline," *Irish Echo*, February 16, 2011.

It was a small school: Brazil, e-mail interview, March 18, 2013.

There was recognition: *Irish Echo*, ibid.

I wanted to spend: Brazil interview, ibid.

I think after: *Irish Echo*, ibid.

The campus has been: Brazil interview, ibid.

I was being: Brazil, "More Engineers in Hard Hats and Heels," *New York Times*, January 17, 2001.

Eventually you find: Brazil interview, ibid.

One thing about: "Galway's Aine Brazil Leaves Her Mark on City's Skyline," ibid.

LANDSCAPE ARCHITECTURE

a gardener: Schuyler Van Rensselaer, *Art Out-of-Doors: Hints on Good Taste in Gardening*, New York, 1893, 18.

Unless a woman: Marian Coffin and Mary Bronson Hartt, "Women and the Art of Landscape Gardening," *Outlook* 88, March 28, 1908 (Outlook Company, 1908), 703.

A woman will fuss: Guy Lowell, *Outlook*, 699.

In terms of fame: Deborah Nevins, "The Triumph of Flora: Women and the American Landscape, 1890–1935," *Antiques*, April 1985, 905.

Beatrix Jones Farrand

A clever child: Jones, Mary Cadwalader, *Lantern Slides*, Boston: Merrymount Press, 1937, 121–122.

A landscape gardener: Van Rensselaer, Mariana Griswold, *Art Out-of-Doors: Hints on Good Taste in Gardening* (New York: Scribner, 1893), 18.

Let her be a gardener: John Cadwalader, Mildred Bliss, "An Attempted Evocation of a Personality," *Beatrix Farrand, Plant Book for Dumbarton Oaks* (Washington, DC: Dumbarton Oaks Trustees for Harvard University, 1980), xxi.

Possibly what first: "Miss Beatrix Jones's Vocation: She Does Landscape Gardening of All Kinds from the Ground Up," *New York Sun*, October 31, 1897, 5.

Will you pardon me: Letter, Fred F. McLain (FFM), College Comptroller to Farrand, January 4, 1940.

lies very close to my heart: Letter, Farrand to McClain, June 14, 1938.

to give the campus: Farrand notes, February 1, 1940.

Dumbarton Oaks: Bliss, Mildred, "An Attempted Evocation of a Personality," *Beatrix Jones Farrand, 1872–1959: An Appreciation of a Great Landscape Gardener* (Washington, DC: Dumbarton Oaks, 1960), 17.

By hiring Mr. Venturi: "New Dumbarton Library: Venturi's Way," *Washington Times*, Friday, March 17, 2006.

in order to have good: Jones Farrand, "The Garden as a Picture," *Scribner's Magazine* 8:4 (July 1907), 2.

Ellen Biddle Shipman

Dean: "Mrs. Ellen Shipman, Landscape Designer," obituary, *New York Times*, March 29, 1950, 29.

Oh! Mama: Biddle, Ellen McGowan, *Reminiscences of a Soldier's Wife* (Philadelphia: J. B. Lippincott, 1907), 11.

Just a few feet below: Ibid., 136.

If you can do: Foreword, Garden Note Book (partial contents in box 10, folder 15, Cornell; hereafter cited as GNB), 1–2.

Working daily: Mary Caroline Crawford, "Homes and Gardens of Cornish," *House Beautiful*, April 1906, 12–14.

I like the outcome: Foreword, *Garden Note Book*, 3–4.

There is no profession: Judith Tankard, *The Gardens of Ellen Biddle Shipman* (Sagapress, 1996), 76.

Before women took: Anne Peterson, "Women Take the Lead in Landscape Art," *New York Times*, March 13, 1938.

Marian Cruger Coffin

Simplicity is: Cruger Coffin, "Garden of Mrs. Vivian Spencer," *Garden Magazine*, August 1922, 368.

I secretly cherished: M. C. Coffin's letter to Clarence Fowler for his article "Three Women in Landscape Architecture," Cambridge School of Architecture and Landscape Architecture *Alumnae Review* 9 (1932): 11.

Unless a woman: Cruger Coffin, Coffin to Fowler, "Three Women in Landscape Architecture," *Cambridge School of Architecture and Landscape Architecture Alumnae Review*, vol. 4, April 1932, 7.

One day I: Hutcheson, Martha Brookes, *The Spirit of the Garden* (University of Massachusetts Press, 2001), Introduction.

In taking up the problem: Cruger Coffin, "A Suburban Garden Six Years Old," *Country Life in America*, vol. 21, no. 8, February 15, 1912, 19–22.

My dear Harry: Cruger Coffin to du Pont, April 25, 1910, Winterthur Archives.

Father would take: Louise, Charles A. Platt, *Italian Gardens* (Harper Brothers, 1884), 37.

the driveway: du Pont to Coffin, May 21, 1929.

the oldest garden: *Horticulture*, vol. 15, no. 16, August 15, 1937.

It was considered: Hutcheson, Hutcheson to Fowler, "Three Women in Landscape Architecture," 9.

Cornelia Hahn Oberlander

What is the green?: Hahn Oberlander, Kathy Stinson, *Love Every Leaf: The Life of Landscape Architect Cornelia Hahn* (Tundra Books, 2008), 8, 9.

He could as: Ibid., 9.

With columns: Grandmother Hahn, Ibid., 13.

I am absolutely certain: Hahn Oberlander, Interview with Charles A. Birnbaum. *Pioneers of American Landscape Design: Cornelia Hahn Oberlander Oral History Interview* (Cultural Landscape Foundation, 2008), 14.

I'm working on: Peter Oberlander, *Love Every Leaf*, 23.

It's too bad: Hahn Oberlander, *Love Every Leaf*, 25.

If kids don't: Ibid., 29.
A playground without: Ibid., 32.
at it's best: Ibid., 46.

Carol R. Johnson

My 11-year-old brother: Oral history interview with Charles A. Birn-
    baum. *Landscape Legends: Carol Johnson Oral History Interview* (Cul-
    tural Landscape Foundation, 2006).
We lit a bonfire: Ibid.
a sort of intimate place: Ibid.
I learned from all the students: Ibid.
TAC was pretty nifty for women: Ibid.
I was terrorized because: Ibid.
I had a hard time: *Landscape Architect*, December 2010.
I want to make: Oral history interview, 2006.
You can learn: Ibid.
I am surprised at: *Landscape Architect*, December 2010.
I always knew: Nitsch phone interview, July 12, 2012.

Martha Schwartz

I was completely: Schwartz, Tim Richardson, ed., *The Vanguard Land-
    scapes and Gardens of Martha Schwartz* (Thanes & Hudson, 2004), 84.
I was so knocked out: Schwartz, Leslie McGuire and Nicole Martin,
    "The Dualities of Reinventing Space," Landscape Online.com.
The use of light: Ibid.
Although my interests: Ibid.

BIBLIOGRAPHY

Allaback, Sarah. *The First American Women Architects*. Urbana: University of Illinois Press, 2008.

American Society of Landscape Architects. "Interview with Martha Schwartz." *The Dirt*. November 15, 2011.

Anthony, Kathryn H. *Designing for Diversity: Gender, Race, and Ethnicity in the Architectural Profession*. Urbana: University of Illinois Press, 2001.

Bennett, Helen Christine. "Kate Gleason's Adventures in a Man's Job." *American Magazine*, October 1928, 42–43, 168–175.

Berkeley, Ellen Perry, ed. *Architecture: A Place for Women*. Washington: Smithsonian Institution Press, 1989.

Bethune, Louise. "Women and Architecture." *Inland Architect and News Record* 17 (March 1891), 21.

Biddle, Ellen McGowan. *Reminiscences of a Soldier's Wife*. Philadelphia: J. B. Lippincott, 1907.

Boutelle, Sara Holmes. *Julia Morgan, Architect*. New York: Abbeville Press, 1988.

Brown, Jane Roy. "Going the Distance." *Landscape Architecture*, December 2010, 28–31.

Chappell, Eve. "Kate Gleason Careers." *Woman Citizen*, January 1926, 19–20, 37–38.

Davis, Heather A. "Thinking Big, Penn Current." University of Pennsylvania, March 26, 2009.

Deitz, Paula. *Of Gardens: Selected Essays.* Philadelphia: University of Pennsylvania Press, 2011.

Des Jardins, Julie. *Lillian Gilbreth: Redefining Domesticity.* Boulder, CO: Westview Press, 2013.

Ehrhart-Morrison, Dorothy. *No Mountain High Enough: Secrets of Successful African American Women.* Berkeley, CA: Conari Press, 1997.

Farrand, Beatrix. *The Collected Writings of Beatrix Farrand: American Landscape Gardener, 1872–1959.* Lebanon, NH: University Press of New England, 2009.

Filler, Martin. *Makers of Modern Architecture: From Frank Lloyd Wright to Frank Gehry.* New York: New York Review Books, 2007.

Fleming, Nancy. *Money, Manure & Maintenance: Ingredients for Successful Gardens of Marian Coffin, Pioneer Landscape Architect, 1876–1957.* Weston, MA: Country Place Books, 1995.

Gabor, Andrea. *Einstein's Wife: Work and Marriage in the Lives of Five Great Twentieth-Century Women.* New York: Penguin, 1995.

Gilbreth, Lillian Moller. *As I Remember.* Norcross, GA: Engineering and Manufacturing Press, 1998.

Glancy, Jonathan. "I Don't Do Nice." *Guardian* (London), October 8, 2006.

Gleason, Janis. *The Life and Letters of Kate Gleason.* Rochester: RIT Press, 2010.

Goff, Alice C. *Women Can Be Engineers.* Michigan: Edwards Brothers, 1946.

Griffin, Marion Mahony. *The Magic of America* (electronic edition). August 2007. The Art Institute of Chicago and the New York Historical Society. October 29, 2008.

Hadid, Zaha, and Aaron Betsky. *Zaha Hadid: Complete Works.* New York: Rizzoli, 2009.

Harris, Gloria G. and Hannah S. Cohen. *Women Trailblazers of California: Pioneers to the Present.* Charleston: History Press, 2012.

Hatch, Sybil E. *Changing Our World: True Stories of Women Engineers.* Reston, VA: American Society of Civil Engineers, 2006.

Horton, Inge S. *Early Women of the San Francisco Bay Area: The Lives and Work of Fifty Professionals.* Jefferson, NC: McFarland and Company, 2010.

Julia Morgan Architectural History Project Interviews: [electronic resource] oral history transcript/tape recorded interview conducted 1974–75.

Johnson, Carol. Interview with Charles A. Birnbaum. *Landscape Legends: Carol Johnson Oral History Interview.* Cultural Landscape Foundation, 2006.

Kahn, Louis I. *Louis Kahn to Anne Tyng: The Rome Letters, 1953–1954.* Edited with commentary by Anne Griswold Tyng. New York: Rizzoli International Publications, Inc., 1997.

Karson, Robin. *A Genius for Place: American Landscapes of the Country Place Era.* Amherst: University of Massachusetts Press, 2007.

Killough-Miller, Joan. "Paving the Way." *Transformations* (Spring 2008).

Lancaster, Jane. *Making Time: Lillian Moller Gilbreth—A Life Beyond "Cheaper by the Dozen."* Boston: Northeastern University Press, 2004.

Latimer, Margaret, ed. with Brooke Hindle and Melvin Kranzberg. *Bridge to the Future: A Centennial Celebration of the Brooklyn Bridge.* New York: New York Academy of Sciences, 1984.

Layne, Margaret E., P.E., ed. *Women in Engineering: Pioneers and Trailblazers.* Reston, VA: American Society of Civil Engineers, 2009.

Macdonald, Anne L. *Feminine Ingenuity: Women and Invention in American.* New York: Ballantine Books, 1992.

Martone, Fran. *In Wright's Shadow: Artists and Architects at the Oak Park Studio.* Oak Park, IL: Frank Lloyd Wright Home and Studio Foundation, 1998.

McCullough, David. *The Great Bridge: The Epic Story of the Building of the Brooklyn Bridge.* New York: Simon and Schuster, 1972.

McKinley, Stephen. "Galway's Aine Brazil Leaves Her Mark on City's Skyline." *Irish Echo,* February 16, 2011.

Mozingo, Louise A. and Linda Jewell, ed. *Women in Landscape Architecture: Essays on History and Practice.* Jefferson, NC: McFarland & Company, 2012.

Oral history interview with Denise Scott Brown, October 25, 1990–November 9, 1991, Archives of American Art, Smithsonian Institution.

Oral history interview with Natalie de Blois, Interviewed by Betty J. Blum, *Chicago Architects Oral History Project,* Ernest R. Graham Study Center for Architectural Drawings Department of Architecture, Art Institute of Chicago, 2004.

Oberlander, Cornelia Hahn. Interview with Charles A. Birnbaum. *Pioneers of American Landscape Design: Cornelia Hahn Oberlander Oral History Interview.* Cultural Landscape Foundation, 2008.

Petrash, Antonia. *More Than Petticoats: Remarkable New York Women.* Guilford, CT: Globe Pequot Press, 2002.

Richardson, Tim. *Avant Gardeners: 50 Visionaries of the Contemporary Landscape.* New York: Thames & Hudson, 2008.

Richardson, Tim, ed. *The Vanguard Landscapes and Gardens of Martha Schwartz.* New York: Thames & Hudson, 2004.

Rothschild, Joan, ed. *Design and Feminism: Re-visioning Spaces, Places, and Everyday Things.* New Brunswick, NJ: Rutgers University Press, 1999.

Royal, Weld. "More Engineers in Hard Hats and Heels." *New York Times,* January 17, 2001.

Schnapp, Ruth Gordon. "Interview with Deborah Rice." Society of Women Engineers, 2006.

Stinson, Kathy. *Love Every Leaf: The Life of Landscape Architect Cornelia Hahn.* New York: Tundra Books, 2008.

Tankard, Judith. *Beatrix Farrand: Private Gardens, Public Landscapes.* New York: Monacelli Press, 2009.

Tankard, Judith. *The Gardens of Ellen Biddle Shipman.* Sagaponack, NY: Sagapress, 1996.

Torre, Susan, ed. *Women in American Architecture: A Historic and Contemporary Perspective.* New York: Whitney Library of Design, 1977.

Tyng, Anne. *Louis Kahn to Anne Tyng: The Rome Letters, 1953–1954.* New York: Rizzoli, 1997.

Van Sweden, James, with Thomas Christopher. *The Artful Garden: Creative Inspiration for Landscape Design.* New York: Random House, 2011.

Van Zanten, David. *Marion Mahony Reconsidered*. Chicago: University of Chicago Press, 2011.

Watson, Anne, ed. *Beyond Architecture: Marion Mahony and Walter Burley Griffin*. Sydney: Powerhouse Publishing, 1998.

Way, Thaisa. *Unbounded Practice: Women and Landscape Architecture in the Early Twentieth Century*. Charlottesville: University of Virginia Press, 2009.

Weigold, Marilyn E. *Silent Builder: Emily Warren Roebling and the Brooklyn Bridge*. New York: Associated Faculty Press, 1984.

Weingardt, Richard. *Engineering Legends: Great American Civil Engineers (Profiles of Inspiration and Achievement)*. Reston, VA: American Society of Civil Engineers, 2005.

Willard, Frances E, and Mary A. R. Livermore. *A Woman of the Century: Fourteen Hundred-Seventy Biographical Sketches Accompanied by Portraits of Leading American Women in All Walks of Life*. Buffalo, NY: Charles Wells Moulton, 1893.

Willis, Beverly, Shiromi Arserio, Meg Pinto, Timothy Sakamoto, Josh Sklair, François Morin, Lois D. Gottlieb, Jane Duncombe, and Eleanore Pettersen. *100 Women Architects in the Studio of Frank Lloyd Wright: Volume 1*. New York: Beverly Willis Architecture Foundation, 2009.

Wilson, Mark Anthony. *Julia Morgan: Architect of Beauty*. Layton, UT: Gibbs Smith Publishers, 2012.

Wood, Debora, ed. *Marion Mahony Griffin: Drawing the Form of Nature*. Evanston, IL: Northwestern University Press, 2005.

Woods, Mary N. *From Craft to Profession: The Practice of Architecture in Nineteenth-Century America*. Berkeley: University of California Press, 1999.

Yost, Edna. *Frank and Lillian Gilbreth: Partners for Life*. New Brunswick, NJ: Rutgers University Press, 1949.

Zink, Clifford W. *The Roebling Legacy*. Princeton, NJ: Princeton Landmark Publications, 2011.

INDEX

Made in the USA
Monee, IL
24 January 2024